Letters
to a
Protestant
Friend

Letters to a Protestant Friend

~Why I Became Catholic~

By

HUGO KLAPPROTH

Foreword
BY MICHAEL J. MATT

Translated from the German
BY DR. JOHN RAO

THE REMNANT PRESS

Dedication

To the memory of the German-American newspapermen who fought to preserve the Faith of our Fathers through the Catholic press apostolate.

Requiescant in pace.

Original German Edition, 1895: *Der Wanderer*, St. Paul, MN
First English Edition, 2022: *The Remnant*

The Remnant Press
PO Box 1117
Forest Lake, Minnesota 55025
www.RemnantNewspaper.com
Copyright © 2022

ISBN: 979-8-218-09476-8

Table of Contents

Foreword by Michael J. Matt vii

Catholicism is Confused Foolishness 1

Catholicism Is Not True Religion 3

On the Worship of the Virgin Mary 6

On the Evil That Is the Jesuits 19

Black Robes and Black Legends 26

A Lutheran Defense of the Society of Jesus 35

Saved by Faith Alone 43

The Sacrament of Confession: A Manmade Insult to Jesus Christ 49

Purgatory: Anti-Biblical Blasphemy 63

Faith? Yes. Reason? No! 73

Catholic Intolerance and the Spanish Inquisition 79

Tolerance: The Child of the Reformation 85

Sola Scriptura (The Bible Alone) 99

Popes & Papists, Popery & Poppycock 114

Sinful Shepherds and their Unholy Catholic Church 122

Miracles: No Such Thing! 133

Christianity Is Not the Catholic Church 141

Reformed Christianity vs. Apostolic Christianity 147

Hugo Klapproth
1848-1919

Foreword by Michael J. Matt

It is my pleasure to reintroduce my great-grandfather Hugo Klapproth and his "new" book, *Letters to a Protestant Friend*. Full disclosure: The book is new only to English-speaking readers living 130 years after it was published in the original German here in St. Paul, Minnesota.

Apart from being a thoughtful historical sketch, this little book also makes a considerable contribution to Catholic apologetics. As a convert from Lutheranism and a professional newspaper editor, Hugo Klapproth's apologetical arguments to his Lutheran friend are some of the most effective I have ever read. *Mary "worship," Faith alone, sola scriptura, the papacy, the "non-biblical" roots of purgatory, and the Sacrament of Confession*—all the go-to Protestant arguments are refuted with expert biblical exegesis, considerable historical acumen, and the patient reproach of one old friend to another.

So, who was Hugo Klapproth?

For me, he was a faded photo on the living room wall of my childhood home—Great-grandfather Klapproth, who had died a half-century ago. My knowledge of his life was limited to old photographs and a short list of biographical points, i.e., born in Germany in 1848, emigrated to America in 1875, died in Lucerne, Switzerland, on September 3, 1919.

I became far better acquainted with my great-grandfather only recently, through the book you are about to read. I was introduced to these letters in 2021, when my daughter dug up a copy of her great-great-grandfather's book in the original German. We had it translated into English and then proceeded to spend the next little while getting to know Hugo Klapproth.

This little book was completed on New Year's Eve, 1894, just before midnight. How do we know that? Grandfather Klapproth tells us so in the last chapter:

It has grown late as I have worked on this letter. Outside, the midnight bells are ringing in the New Year; 1895 A.D. Will this year bring to you, my friend, peace, and true happiness? Will it lead you home to the mother abandoned by your and my forefathers?

Through his letters, Hugo Klapproth has been recalled to life. In my mind's eye, I can now see my great-grandfather sitting at his desk, writing by the light of his oil lamp, which my great-grandmother fills only partway: "My beloved wife," writes Great-grandfather Klapproth in Chapter 4, "in order to prevent me from writing past midnight, has given me so little oil for my lamp that the light is now about to go out right under my nose. Wives are like that—full of 'Jesuitical tricks'…"

He had a sense of humor, obviously…he was Catholic! And there he sits, smiling in his dimly lit study a century ago, teasing his wife, and trying to coax an old friend into the loving embrace of Mother Church. He wrote the letters in his spare time, he tells us, in the evenings, after coming home from work. Eventually, he bound them and entitled the collection, *Briefe an einen protestantischen Freund* (*Letters to a Protestant Friend*)— the book you're about to read.

A little historical context may here be in order:

Hugo's grandson—my father, Walter L. Matt—founded the traditional Catholic newspaper, *The Remnant*, in 1967. The "parent paper" of *The Remnant* is the oldest Catholic weekly newspaper in America, *The Wanderer*, founded a hundred years before, in 1867 by two Benedictine monks at the Assumption Church in St. Paul, Minnesota. Though not newspaper men themselves, they had founded *Der Wanderer* in an attempt to safeguard German immigrants against the ideas of the German "enlightenment"—ideas which would eventually give rise to Hitler's National Socialism.

After two years of struggling to launch *Der Wanderer*, the monks realized that the project was well beyond their abilities, and so they determined to try to find a professional lay editor to take it over. As it turned out, Great-grandfather Hugo

Klapproth was to become their man.

Born in Zellerfield, Germany, on August 29, 1848, Hugo emigrated to Kentucky before moving his family to Wisconsin, where he worked as editor of the Lutheran daily newspaper, the Milwaukee Germania. He was a respected member of the Missouri Synod Lutheran Church.

Back in Germany, the renowned historian, Father Johannes Janssen, SJ, had just completed a four-volume study of the history of the Reformation in Germany, which was not at all flattering to Lutheranism. Since his reputation as a scholar was considerable even here in America, the Lutheran establishment was anxious to see the Catholic priest's work refuted.

The editors of Germania determined that Hugo Klapproth was best qualified to refute Father Janssen's case against Luther; but during the course of his study, Great-grandfather Klapproth himself became persuaded by Father Janssen's arguments. He informed his editors that they would have to find another man for the job, as he and his entire family were to convert to the Catholic Faith.

News of Hugo Klapproth's conversion reached our two monks up here in St. Paul, and they invited him to take over the struggling *Der Wanderer*. He agreed, and after devoting a few years to building *Der Wanderer* into a thriving enterprise, he realized that he needed an assistant.

That assistant would be Joseph Matt who, like Klapproth, was a German immigrant. Born on October 16, 1877, in Kirrweiler, Germany, he arrived in New York in 1895 at just 17 years of age.

After his graduation from Canisius College, Joseph Matt took a job as a reporter for several German Catholic daily newspapers, first in Buffalo and later in Pittsburgh. His unapologetically Catholic approach to the problems of the day attracted the attention of Hugo Klapproth.

In 1897, my grandfather teamed up with my great-grandfather here in St. Paul, and thus began his life-long service to the Catholic Press Apostolate. In 1899, failing health compelled Klapproth to return to Germany, leaving Joseph Matt behind to take his place as editor.

Joseph returned briefly to Germany that same year to wed Hugo Klapproth's daughter, Marie Klapproth (my grandmother), and that union produced six children, the youngest of whom was Walter, my father, future editor of *The Wanderer* and founder of *The Remnant*.

So, there's the historical context. And now to the book.

Hugo Klapproth's letters are as relevant today as they were in 1895. They provide a window into the past, shedding light on how the Catholic Church was perceived by the non-Catholic world, how she'd accompanied waves of European immigrants, welcomed them, educated them, and made them her own.

Especially these days, when Catholic churchmen are often embarrassed by the pre-Vatican II attitudes, my great-grandfather's autobiographical account of how things actually were helps put the lie to Modernism's revisionist history. In point of fact, the Catholic Church, long before Vatican II, was teeming with vocations, united worldwide by the Latin Mass, maintaining the largest hospital and school systems in the world, and blessed by an endless caravan of converts.

The Catholic Church into which my great-grandfather converted attracted some of the most influential thinkers, activists, and writers of the day, men of letters who found it impossible to ignore the clarion call of Mother Church— converts such as G.K. Chesterton, John Henry Newman, Maruice Baring, Charles Péguy, Robert Hugh Benson, Ronald Knox, Christopher Dawson, Evelyn Waugh, etc.—all drawn by the spiritual and intellectual firepower of the mighty pre-conciliar Catholic Church.

This little book of letters, then, provides an inadvertent indictment of those who would denigrate the Catholic Church of yesterday as an ivory tower inhabited by "rigid neo-Pelagians" who failed to lovingly welcome the people of the world. Nothing could be further from the truth, and my great-grandfather would reject such bigoted revisionism out of hand. Why? Because he himself was one of those "people of the world" whom Holy Mother Church had adopted as one of her own.

How much did this particular German immigrant convert come to love his adoptive mother, the Catholic Church? Read the letters that follow! It's positively palpable in every line.

In the words that follow, we discover arguments—old and new—that remind us that, no matter how sinful her members might be, the Catholic Church will always be the spotless bride of Jesus Christ and, as such, would have been defended by the Catholic converts of yesterday.

Writing 130 years ago, Hugo Klapproth is in fact a traditional Catholic pioneer. The Traditions he defends in his day are the same we defend in ours. The Mass he attends is the same Latin Mass we attend today. The Catholic teachings he champions in 1895 are the same we champion in 2022.

Great-grandfather Klapproth's story, then, as laid out in this little book, again makes it obvious that traditional Catholics today, far from inventing something new, are simply trying to defend the Catholic Faith exactly as it was handed down to them.

Nothing has changed. From his grave, Hugo Klapproth reminds us that even in times of great turmoil, we can never leave Holy Mother Church. We are called by God to stay and to defend her, to survive and to hand down the Faith of our fathers to our sons, exactly as our fathers handed it down to us. Our task remains unchanged.

Michael J. Matt
October 20, 2022

~Chapter 1~
Catholicism is Confused Foolishness

Dear D.,

So, my conversion to the Catholic Church appears to you to be "totally astonishing, incomprehensible, almost unforgivable." You cannot comprehend how I could "become unfaithful to the Faith of our fathers," and to do so "not so as to progress towards still greater freedom, but to return to Roman spiritual slavery"—something that was so abhorrent to me in my youth, as it also was to you. Obviously, you would not dare to ascribe this step to improper motivation. Nevertheless, under the first impression that this "Job-like" message made on you it seemed that our relationship was finished once and for all. You were only able to bring yourself to write to me again after serious hesitation, due to the memory of our friendship of such long duration.

Now, my dear D., first of all, I assure you how thankful I am that you have not broken off your friendship with me. Scarcely any of the many and difficult cares that my heart placed in the way of my will before my entry into the Catholic Church was to oppress me more than the thought that the love and friendship of so many of those whom I knew would be denied me from that hour onwards. As far as I am concerned, I can assure you that I would have remained true to our friendship even if you had forgotten it. Love and friendship have grown ever more important and ever stronger for me in the warm sunshine of a religion that is Catholic, universal, encompasses all and animates all.

Towards the end of your letter, you write: 'I can well imagine that a poetic spirit such as yours might feel drawn to the fragrant incense of Catholic mysticism, the resplendence of the Catholic cult, and the sublime beauty of its old cathedrals. But what is incomprehensible to me is that you, with your

1

clear intelligence and your warm heart, can stomach all of the confused foolishness and uncharitable intolerance of the Roman Church. And—do not take this amiss—I do not believe that you can."

I do not take it amiss. The manner in which you seek to construe my conversion is not new. When Friedrich Leopold von Stolberg, Friedrich von Schlegel and other Protestant Romantics became Catholic, their non-Catholic friends explained this in a totally similar fashion. But they were in error then, just as you are now. As far as my case is concerned, you must believe that my heart and my head were in the most complete harmony when I entered the Catholic Church; that I believe everything that this Church teaches, from the greatest to the smallest truth, firmly and unshakably; that I am fully clear regarding the reasons for which I believe these teachings. Admittedly, were the Catholic Church to be judged by what you understand under that name—and what she once was for me as well as for millions of others, and which she only is according to hearsay and the testimony of her accusers—then, certainly, I would still turn away from her in abhorrence. But she is in general the opposite of this.

Still, I fear that I have already exhausted your interest in this subject. For, from what I have heard, you are said recently to have become rather indifferent to religious questions. And however much I would indeed regret this were it to be true, I do not feel that it is my task to preach to someone who is unwilling to listen. God will provide!

Let us therefore keep our correspondence in the future on rather more neutral territory.

With all love, your H.

~Chapter 2~
Catholicism Is Not True Religion

Dear D.,

Contrary to my expectation, you have come back once again to the question of my conversion, and have even dedicated the greatest part of your letter to it. As a result, you do not seem to me to belong to the category of the completely indifferent. Yes, you do indeed write that what a man believes basically does not concern you; that, in fact, you consider every religious viewpoint to be worthy of respect if only it be based upon honest conviction. And that, of course, is a manner of speech popular to indifferentism as such.

However, you certainly cannot be fully serious about this. For although you yourself now repeatedly assure me that you do not in the slightest doubt the sincerity of my "new convictions," you are very zealously endeavoring to convince me that Catholicism is not the true religion. Where does so much zeal come from, if every religious conviction—and, therefore, Catholic convictions as well—seem worthy of respect to you?

Incidentally, your objections remind me of a dictum of the convert, Freiherr L. von Hammerstein, in his work, *Recollections of an old Lutheran* (page 72): "Actually, my experience has been that Protestants engaged in controversies with Catholics almost always go about their work in a negative rather than a positive way. Their statements almost always are limited to the claim that the Catholic Church is not the true Church; that she does not possess a pure Christianity. Such a procedure reminds me of the definition that Mephistopheles gave of himself: 'I am the Spirit that always negates.'"

Among the reasons that you offer as to why Catholicism is supposedly not the true religion, is its "barbaric claim" to be the only true one, as a result of which, as you understand it, all non-Catholics are damned. There is, additionally, that "mad doctrine" of Papal Infallibility, which, among other things, "threatens nations with a tutelage at the hands of the Roman Priest-King, compelling non-Catholics to be continually on their guard, and, as a result, provoking them to endless Culture Wars." Furthermore, there is "the incomprehensible deification of humanity found in the Marian cult and in that of the Saints" and the "well known Jesuit maxim of the end justifying the means," which "one is obliged to ascribe to the Church as well, since she does not condemn the Jesuits for it, but rather still holds them in high honor."

What I learn from all this, dear D., is that "you have learned nothing and forgotten nothing" since our school years, and especially since our religious instruction under good old Rector Z., who was an excellent philologist but who had not studied theology. The points that you cite are certainly truly "barbaric," "mad" and the like, so much so that no rational man, and particularly no Christian, could find them acceptable. And if these were indeed doctrines of the Catholic Church, they would most probably have to be laid at the feet of her followers, who were "barbaric," "mad" and otherwise limited poor souls, and were so from time immemorial.

But gunpowder, therefore, presumably could not have been invented before the Reformation, nor the art of printing, nor the Copernican worldview, nor could the *Song of the Niebelungen* or the *Divine Comedy* ever have been written. These were achievements that thrilled our Rector Z.—who looked with such contempt upon everything Catholic—to the seventh heaven.

And then one has to deal with Windthorst {the leader of the Catholic Centre Party} and Leo XIII, Manning and Newman, Johannes Janssen and F.W. Weber, none of whom Protestants, despite their general indifference, deny possessing a serious higher education. I suppose they should also be counted among the ninnies. Or, perhaps, they should be placed in the category of the deplorable hypocrites? Dear God, there are not lacking those filled with blind hatred for Rome who seek to convince themselves even of this, although I do not think that you are to be counted among them. If it were otherwise, I would not enter into any discussion with you at all.

In conclusion, let me offer you my certainty that if your objections truly touched upon doctrines of the Catholic Church, this Church would continue to have scarcely a more resolute opponent than myself.

Your H.

~Chapter 3~
On the Worship of the Virgin Mary

Dear D.,

You regret that my answers have turned out to be so "tight-lipped." Since you have brought this matter up once again, you would, after all, like "to know something more about it."

Dear D., I cannot help but confess that I do not speak with you regarding these questions without a certain amount of reluctance. For I fear stirring up doubt in your soul. I fear that since I do not know whether through arousing such doubt you will reach clarity, or, if, with the grace of God, that clarity should come about, you would then willingly follow up this enlightenment. For, as our Schiller has his Cassandra say: "Life is only error; and knowledge is death."

There is something true in that statement insofar as it is better to err due to no fault of one's own than to know the truth without following up on its serious call. Consequently, in accordance with a thoroughly Catholic principle, I have generally taken it as a rule not to enter into religious controversies unnecessarily with those who believe differently. But you ask, and to your questions answers should be given.

No, my good D., your conception of the only true Church is utterly wrong. Admittedly, you share this with the great mass of Protestants, although any Catholic Catechism could easily give anyone better instruction on the topic. So here follows the desired "enlightenment."

Catholics do not believe that Protestants who are baptized and without any fault of their own find themselves outside the Catholic Church are excluded from Heaven: provided that they believe in the Triune God, that God will reward the good and punish the evil, that Jesus Christ is the Son of God, our Savior and sole intermediary, and that if they have offended God, they sincerely repent of their sins. Augustine says, "all those who adhere to a belief, even though false and perverse, but do not stubbornly defend it— having received it from parents who were already misled and in a state of error—and who diligently strive for the Truth and are prepared to recognize it when they find it, are in no way to be counted among the heretics" (Augustine, *Epistle*, CLXII).

If, however, such persons are to be found among the blessed in Heaven, it is not their "Church" that is responsible, for solely the one and only Catholic Church of Jesus Christ is able to put them there. Catholics believe that Protestants of the type described above are not in spirit Protestants at all, but Catholics, even if they themselves do not know it. They believe that these Christians belong to the "soul" of the Church, although they are not linked through external union with the "body" of the Church.

In order to repeat the point explicitly, they believe this of such Protestants, if they, without any guilt of their own, live cut off from the "body" of the Church, and having no doubt that their Faith is the correct one, have no means at all to learn of the true religion, or find that their honest efforts to discover this religion are unsuccessful. It is different, however, when an "invincible ignorance," as the Church calls it, is *not* present; if, that is to say, someone has, but does not use, the opportunity to come to know the true religion, or, if he, upon recognizing it, in defiance of the voice of his conscience, does not confess the truth that has been discerned; perhaps, as so often happens, due to earthly considerations. Here, error obviously becomes serious sin, and he who persists in serious sin until death personally hands himself over to eternal doom.

You see, dear D., the teaching of the sole redemptive Church is not in fact as uncharitable and barbaric as you imagine it, unless the words of Christ Himself were necessarily uncharitable and barbaric: "He who believes and is baptized will be saved; he who does not believe will be damned."

Your conception of infallibility—which is based upon Bismarck, as clearly emerges through the conclusions you derive from it—is just as erroneous. The Catholic does not believe that the pope is infallible in everything that he prescribes or decides. The dogma of Infallibility relates only to theological decisions of the Pope, and, indeed, even these are very far from all of them being infallible. It is only when the pope speaks, *ex cathedra*, i.e., as the highest Church authority to whom the whole Church turns in order for those truths which are contained in the Deposit of Revelation to be enunciated, that he is validly presumed by us to be infallible. He can err in earthly sciences, and, yes, even in theology when he treats of this as a private scholar.

And it is similar with respect to his moral life. It crosses no Catholic's mind to consider the pope to be sinless. When the news of the death of Pius IX reached the United States, an Irish-American priest in Fredericksburg, Virginia, passed it on to his congregation and added: "If he died as a Christian, then he will be among the blessed; if he did not, then not. Let us pray for his poor soul!" I would not maintain that this remark was particularly tactful; simply that it corresponds completely to the Catholic understanding of the pope.

The pope can also in no way add anything new to the Deposit of Faith; i.e., something that was not already in Divine Revelation. If, therefore, the pope, or the Church, renders a decision regarding the Faith, this is still only a solemn confirmation or a clearer exposition of a teaching that was at least already implicitly taught within her community going back to the days of the Apostles: irrespective of whether individual Catholics may have been clear regarding this doctrine beforehand, or may even actually have doubted it.

I know very well that not only theoretical but also historical objections have been raised against the dogma of the Infallibility of the pope. Msgr. J. Schröder, a German Professor at Catholic University in Washington, D.C., recently gave a short but impressive answer to such objections in a lecture on the Papacy. Here, he stated:

> You need not remind us of the good-natured and all too unwary Honorius I, who did not confront decisively

enough the heresy of the Monothelites, allowing himself to be deceived by the crafty Byzantine Patriarch, Sergius. Consequently, both Pope Leo II, one of his successors, as well as the Sixth General Council, very sharply rebuked his docile, blind confidence.

You can just as little trouble us or make us anxious with reference to Pope Vigilius. We will happily admit that even the unprecedentedly difficult situation in which he found himself does not protect him sufficiently against the reproach of inconstancy. Furthermore, we do not need you to teach us that Stephen VI and John XXII personally paid their homage to positions that any textbook of theology today would designate as being thoroughly false.

We know just as well as you do that a Roman Congregation did not understand the system of Galileo, which contradicted the concepts then reigning everywhere, and therefore expressly rejected it. We will in no way give pause to stating along with you that certain popes did not make political decisions prompted by the sharp eye of a Richelieu or a Bismarck, and were even sometimes downright far off the mark. This is nowhere better indicated and proven than in the magnificent *History of the Papacy* of Ludwig von Pastor. In spite of that, we are proud of this worthy disciple of our great Janssen.

All these objections have nothing to do with Papal Infallibility, and above all else, cannot put into question for a moment any of the pope's supernatural prerogatives. You must prove to us that a given pope at a given time—be he named Alexander VI or Pius IX, John XXII or Leo XIII or any other among the two hundred sixty popes—ever obliged the whole Church to accept an error as a revealed Truth; or that a pope, as the messenger of the Law of Christ, as a guide of souls to heaven, ever called vice a virtue, or virtue a vice.

Yes, I can go still further. Show to us any pope

whomsoever who ever canonized anyone who did not live as a saint or at least die as a saint; that any pope whomsoever solemnly approved the constitutions or the statutes of a religious order despite the fact that these statutes were in contradiction to true moral standards. Or, in order to give you an easy means of exploiting and tossing out all of our arguments, that any one pope, whomsoever he may be, ever permitted a Philip August of France, a Henry IV of Germany, a Henry VIII of England, or anyone whomsoever, even at the price of losing an entire kingdom, to repudiate his legitimate wife to marry another woman. Give us some proof of that sort, and we will declare together with you that it is not only the natural weaknesses of men that come to light in the history of the Papacy, but also that the popes never received from Christ our Lord the supernatural prerogatives recognized by us Catholics; or, if they ever had possessed them, that from that unfortunate moment onwards their possession vanished from this Earth, and with them the Church of Christ.

I now come to the "deification of man in the Catholic cult of Mary and in that of the Saints." To deify someone doubtless means to place him on the same level as God, to bestow divine honors to him, to adore him. Do you really think that we Catholics do not know the First Commandment? Honestly, that means that if one charges us with divinizing Mary and the saints, we Catholic not only deny all of Christianity, but that we also degrade ourselves in the sight of the Jews and the Moslems. Admittedly, we venerate her and we venerate them, but in the measure that God Himself cherishes the both of them.

Above all, with respect to Mary, it should indeed be clear to every Bible-believing Protestant that God did not cherish anyone among all his creatures more than He cherished her. This should be obvious. The fact that this actually is *not* the case is proven, as so often, by the irreverent manner in which Mary is spoken of in the pages of Protestant books and even from orthodox Protestant pulpits.

A clear-seeing Protestant says when addressing this point:

> There is a relationship of consistent flight from the Mother of God, a constant fear of her, or of even uttering but a word of the greeting that the Eternal Father sent to her through the mouth of an angel, thereby issuing the first blow against the old curse separating us from Him and His love. We are permitted to call out an *ave pia anima* as often as we want to any other human person who has gone before us to our eternal home, but not to the Mother of Christ, because that would be—Catholic! (Dietlein, *Evang. Ave Maria*, Halle, 1863, VII).

I can assure you that the Protestant disrespect for Mary alone would now be sufficient to prove to me that Protestantism cannot be the religion of Jesus Christ. "Every heresy has always ended with a contempt for the Virgin" (Hettinger, *Apol.*, Freiburg, 1869, II, 1, 529). No, whoever sees and honors the Bible as the true Word of God must look upon and honor in Mary that "blessed among women"; and he must "laud her as blessed through all generations" until the end of time.

In truth, the veneration of Mary is so natural for the Christian who is logical in his belief; it is so completely understandable for every true disciple of her Divine Son, that only a total blindness could misjudge it.

> If I call upon the name of Jesus,
> I can never speak to Him alone,
> After 'Jesus' I call upon 'Mary'
> Think first of Him and then of Her!
> Who, indeed, is he who separates Mother and Child,
> Who after all are so closely bound together?
> You who bore for us the Son of God,
> Remain for us forever Mother.

By chance, an American leaflet came into my possession today that illustrates the rationality of the Catholic veneration of Mary in a very simple although no less accurate manner. And because Protestantism has impressed upon us precisely such an irrational caricature of the Catholic Marian cult, I wanted to cite a passage from this here:

The Fourth of July takes first place among all the civil holidays of this land. It is the day on which the freedom of this country was born; the day in the year 1776 when a number of excellent, noble and freedom-loving men gathered together in Philadelphia and signed a document which announced to the crowned head of England that the colonists were tired of British tutelage and tyranny and that they were breaking away from it. And so the dawn of freedom broke forth across this entire land.

This day is justly celebrated in a splendid way on account of that fact. Businesses are closed, everywhere one hears the joyful and jubilant shouts of the people, everywhere resound rifles and pistols and the thunder of cannon. In the cities, brilliant parades are held; soldiers in gala uniforms move with shining guns and pistols, accompanied by drum rolls and star-spangled banners through the densely animated streets. In the evening the cities glow with innumerable stars reflecting the manifold colors of the bonfires and the shooting off of rockets. The rattling of the fireworks seem as though they will never come to an end. The houses of the citizens sport festive decorations. A number of homes are emblazoned with the portrait of a noble man who is justly known to every American under the name of the Father of his Country. Not infrequently, one sees next to the painting of this man that of a woman as well. And if one asks who this woman might be, the answer is that she is the mother of George Washington.

Let us imagine someone who might be angered over the display of that picture, mock it, and ask why it was being publicly displayed.After all, what had she done for the country? Had she led the American Army? Did she draw up the battle lines and lead the troops to victory? Did she plunge into the fray with a weapon in her hand to strike the cocky British on the head? No, the answer would be; nothing of the sort. She was nothing more than a common woman, an everyday housewife. 'Therefore, down with the picture', the critic might cry out!

What would one say to such a man? Is it not true that he would be told that he had lost his reason and had gone mad? What if he went further; if he picked up stones and mud to hurl at and dishonor and soil the picture of this truly fine and noble woman; what then? Is it not true that in less than no time a hundred hands would rise to avenge the scandal, and the evildoer would later tell of his good fortune if he had managed to get out of the situation by the skin of his teeth?

But who is this woman, this mother, in comparison with the Mother of God? Who is her son, on whose account she is honored, in comparison with the Son of Mary, who freed not only one land, one people, but the peoples and the nations and the men of all lands and of all times, and freed them not from the tyranny of an earthly power, but from the slavery and the dominion of the devil? This woman is someone who re-opened the gates of heaven closed to us through sin and destroyed the sentence of our rejection; a woman who made us the children of the Father of her Son, who is the Lord, God, Creator, and Guide of all things, and His own co-heirs. How ineffably high and exalted must Mary now stand above all other mothers, since her Son so infinitely towers above all other sons of men!

If an ordinary mother, whose son is respected and has become famous through heroic deeds which he earned on behalf of the well-being of his fellow citizens and his Fatherland, and whose mother is therefore not permitted to be mocked or denigrated or blasphemed or reviled, how much more has Mary earned that highest honor and distinction: she, the Mother of Jesus Christ, the Son of God, who has redeemed the whole human race from its sins; she who was the means by which this Redemption came to pass!

How curious this is! Scarcely did I start writing this letter to you, when the American Press reported the unveiling of a Mary Washington Monument in Fredericksburg, Virginia and the accompanying discourse of President Cleveland. This speech forms a kind of counterpart to what I just noted above. The Protestant speaker said, "I believe that the man who forgets a love for his mother is capable of every treason and every deprivation and cannot be trusted. George Washington said: 'All that I am I owe to my mother.' Therefore, we should never forget that if fame and honor fall due to a man, a share in that fame and that honor is due to his mother." How curious that such an unintended but no less conclusive justification of the Catholic Marian cult should come precisely in this month [May, 1894]; the month that we Catholics are used to dedicating to the special veneration of the mother of our Lord. And, by the way, the mother of Washington was also named Mary.

Still, however much we Catholics honor and distinguish Mary, never has it occurred to us to compare her, a creature, even only distantly, to God; much less to place her on the same level with God. She, for us, is infinitely small and limited with respect to God. We ascribe to her absolutely no power whatsoever other than that which she has obtained from God. And the same holds true for us with respect to the other saints. We pray to God—the Catholic Catechism tells us this—so that He may help us through His Omnipotence; we pray to the saints so that they may help us through their intercession with God.

But can we not see in this prayer a kind of mistrust of Jesus Christ? No, for we expect first of all grace and eternal life from God's will alone, through the merits of Christ. We look, secondly to the intercession of the saints, as well as to those of the angels, as can also be seen in Holy Scriptures themselves, as, for example, in the Revelation of St. John (5:8), where twenty four Elders are said always to be before the Throne of God, unceasingly bringing the prayers of the saints to the All

Highest. The living, also, pray for one another, but does anyone think that this somehow cripples Christ's role as mediator? However, should you doubt that those dwelling in the hereafter know something of us, and if you still consider the Bible to be valid to look to for God's Word, then you can easily rid yourself of your doubt if you would glean the message of still further scriptural passages besides those mentioned above: Luke 13:10; Tobias 12:12; Zacharias 1:12; 2 Maccabees 15:12-15.

Even Luther, although he often contradicts himself in this regard as he does in every other matter as well, has testified to calling upon the aid of the saints. Thus, he once admitted: "I say and hold fast with the whole of Christianity that we should honor and call upon the loving saints; for who would contest that in our day, God, through His Holy Name, still visibly performs miracles at the sites of their holy bodies and graves?" (*Wittenberg* 7, 7). Testimonies to the invocation of the Saints can be found in Luther, albeit alongside contrary statements, until the year 1541; that is to say, five years before his death.

Here is a passage from a splendid apologetic pastoral letter that the Bishops of Prussia addressed to the faithful of their dioceses from the tomb of St. Boniface, in Fulda, in January of 1889. They wrote:

> The crown of all of the distortions of the teachings of the Catholic Faith is the assertion that the Catholic Church… attributes the adoration which is due to God alone to the Virgin Mary and to the saints as well. We reject this assertion with the deepest disgust. We Catholics direct all of our reverence, consisting of our Faith, Hope, Love and Worship, solely and alone to the true, living, Triune God.

> To direct this divine worship to any creature whomsoever, however exalted he or she might be in the order of nature and grace, is idolatry in the eyes of every Catholic. The reverence to God is the sole thing that we call worship. That which we direct to the Mother of God is essentially and totally different. Just as little as the honor and love

that children render to their parents, or subjects to their princes, contradicts the love due to God—it, in fact, fulfills His fourth commandment—does reverence to the saints contradict the worship due only to Him. Rather, this arises from that divine reverence and shares in its same goal. We honor the saints as friends of God, as true followers and members of Christ because God Himself honors them this way as well. However, all honor that we render to them we render on account of God and for the glorification of God, who through His grace sanctified them and gave them to us as a model.

This applies in the highest measure to the reverence that we render to the Most Blessed Virgin in fulfillment of the words: 'Behold, from now on all generations will call me blessed.' For this reverence has its sole ground and its sole goal in Jesus Christ, in whom we believe as the true Son of the Eternal Father and the true Son of the Virgin Mary. In offering such reverence we are far removed from considering Mary as someone other than a creature. Yes, she is the purest and most holy among all creatures, but all of her purity and sanctity have been given to her through the merit and grace of Jesus Christ for His honor. We also honor Mary no differently, no more, and no less than God Himself, according to the witness of the Gospel through the message of the angel, who honored her in greeting her as 'full of grace'; as someone in whom 'the Lord is.'

If we call upon Mary, the angels and the saints, we do not expect grace and help from them due to their own power. Rather, we expect these blessings through their intercession, from God alone, through their and our sole Redeemer, Jesus Christ. Asking the Mother of our Savior and the glorified saints for the help of their prayers is just as reasonable and Christian as our appealing to our fellow Christians on earth for their prayers. If Saint Paul in his epistles asks for the prayers of the faithful, should it therefore be wrong if we commend ourselves to his intercession in Heaven? Or should the 'Our Father' lose its strength due to the fact that we bring the memory of our Salvation in Christ Jesus to Him through the greeting of the angel, and add the petition: 'Holy Mary, Mother of God, prayer for us sinners, now and at the hour of our death?'

Also, we do not ascribe to the saints either omniscience or any other divine characteristic, but rather trust that God will allow them to have our supplications recognized, so that they can continue in Heaven the work of the Christian love that they practiced on the Earth. The Catholic Church teaches that this reasonable and pious recourse to the saints, which emergences directly from the article of the Apostles Creed regarding the Communion of Saints, is salutary and beneficial, and that it applies in a special way to our own age. For it is indeed beneficial and salutary to oppose to the absorption in earthly affairs and the illusions of transient desires models of heavenly feeling; to set against these, holy lives full of self-renunciation and the eternal Kingdom of Christ and his elect that is also our eternal goal.

Now let us turn to "the well-known Jesuit maxim of the end justifying the means." It really pains me that you also bring up with me this sad old hag of an argument from the junk room of anti-Catholic foolishness and malice. Do you honestly not feel that in doing so you are not being deeply insulting and offensive? What else could it be if you ascribe to a friend the thought that he would recognize the Church of the infinitely holy God in a Church that would approve of such an appalling lie; one that says that a good end sanctifies even a bad means?

Listen, my dear D., this is how you can earn yourself a nice heap of money. You can do so by providing the proof that such a diabolical teaching actually does appear in the writings of the Jesuits. Grand prizes for doing so have already been offered, both in the Old as well as in the New Worlds. However, no one up until now has been able to earn them. Perhaps fortune beckons you here. If you succeed in discovering the proof, I will make sure that the payment for your efforts is not held back. But then you would also have to prove how the entire, great, Society of Jesus, and, indeed, how the whole Church, must be held responsible for this erroneous delusion of one of its members, whose existence had up until now remained undiscovered.

In the meantime, your H. greets you.

~Chapter 4~
On the Evil That Is the Jesuits

My Dear D.!

I could have predicted that most of what I wrote to you in my last letter would be "completely new" to you. On the other hand, what is *not* new to *me* is the objection that you cite against the reverence of Mary as a saint. You say that the Mother of Jesus undoubtedly and verifiably sinned, at least once, by leaving her twelve-year old Son behind, alone, in the Temple. If this were true, that would indeed admittedly toss the doctrine of the Immaculate Conception into the rubbish bin, but not that of Mary's saintliness. Paul, Peter, the Magdalene and many others whom the Church reveres as saints were not always sinless. Even the just man falls seven times daily. But it is actually not correct. For if in the case you cite the Mother had sinned, so, doubtless, her Son had done so as well, since He had remained behind in the Temple without the permission of His mother. And, with this, the whole of Christianity would obviously collapse.

With respect to the Jesuits, I was indeed much too brief in my comments. While fully recognizing my good faith in my judgment of "Jesuitical morality" you claim that you cannot convince yourself that "millions among all peoples, who in the course of centuries have opposed this secret order (!!!), learned and honorable men among them, not only Protestant theologians but also great statesmen and historians of different denominations, yes even an infallible Pope, can be said to have erred."

So, since you seem to wish this, I will today expand upon that subject somewhat more fully.

To begin with, there is a no special ethical teaching of the Jesuits; no "Jesuitical morality" at all. The ethical teaching of the Jesuits is the teaching of the Catholic Church. Or do you really think it conceivable that the Church could tolerate in her community an association that taught a morality that was alien to her own? The "millions" of opponents of the Jesuits, and the fact that not all of them were or are uneducated, dishonorable, and of insignificant positions in life, proves nothing against them. Otherwise, one could also justly bring up the same "proof" against Him for whom the Society of Jesus is named. The "infallible" pope that you cite against the Jesuits of course does prove something: namely that you either superficially read or already once again have forgotten my explanation of the meaning of Papal Infallibility. For the fact the Clement XIV suppressed the Society of Jesus has not the least thing to do with Infallibility. This was simply a political act to which the Pope, worn down by illness, anxiety and trepidation due to the influence of the irreligious and unprincipled rulers of Portugal, Spain and France, believed himself compelled to perform. Clement XIV afterwards bitterly regretted this weakness. One often heard him cry out: *"Compulsus sum!"* ("I was forced to do it!").

The fact that you call the Society of Jesus a "secret order" also proves something; but only that this Society is *terra incognita* to you, and that this—excuse me for saying it—should make you shy away from condemning it. It is a generally recognized legal principle that no one must be condemned unheard, no matter how numerous and strident his accusers may be, nor however great the crime imputed to him. The judge who, without himself investigating the action of the accused, would convict someone as a result of a mere hue and clamor, would simultaneously render himself guilty of cruelty and injustice. Should this principle not be valid with respect to the Jesuits as well? Moreover, the Society of Jesus is as little a secret society as your Evangelical Union or the Gustav Adolph Association themselves are. Its Constitution, its writings, its history, its life and its work in our own day are an open book, available for the examination of anyone whomsoever who would undertake the effort.

You express your astonishment that "there is said to be nothing true" regarding the Jesuitical maxim of the end justifying the means, and that you never heard before of the public competition which I mentioned at the conclusion of my previous letter. Consequently, I will come back to this question as well. In the year 1852, at the end of a popular mission in Frankfurt am Main, the Jesuit Father Roh made the following declaration from the pulpit:

1. If anyone from the Faculty of Law of Heidelberg or Bonn can produce a book published by a Jesuit in which, according to the judgment of the faculty, the infamous principle that 'the end justifies the means,' either in these or in synonymous words, may be found, I will, upon being informed of this by the faculty, pay to the person who brings forth that book one thousand Gulden (from Rhein Westphalien).

2. Whoever, on the other hand, orally or in writing, ascribes this ignominious doctrine to the Society of Jesus without having brought forth such a proof, is a dishonorable slanderer.

This declaration was disseminated, and a keen but unsuccessful hunt for such a book began. In 1862, Father Roh repeated his declaration in Halle, and in 1863 in Bremen. Finally, in 1868, an answer came from the Protestant side. The preacher Maurer published in Mannheim a brochure under the following rather sonorous title: *The New Mirror of Jesuits. In Particular the Proof that the Jesuits Teach the Principle: The End Justifies the Means.* He said that the "proof" had been found in Father Busenbaum's *Medulla Theologia Moralis.*

In 1869, Father Roh gave Herr Maurer a thorough piece of his mind in a small work published in Freiburg im Breisgau entitled *The Old Song: The End Justifies the Means.* Here, he proved Maurer's falsification of the text and his violation and misunderstanding of its context. Nevertheless, Maurer made an attempt to get the one thousand Gulden prize from the Faculty of Law of Heidelberg. He abandoned it on the advice of a prudent member of the Faculty. And ever afterwards, no one has yet been able to win it.

In the New World a few years ago, Reverend Joseph Jessing, Director of a higher educational institute and of an orphanage, as well as the editor of a widely diffused weekly journal, the *Ohio Orphans Friend* in Columbus, Ohio, offered a $1,000 prize for the proof that the Jesuits, or merely just one of their moral theologians, ever taught that infamous principle. He maintains that offer still today.

The convert Georg Gotthilf Evers, who was a Lutheran Pastor in the 1870s from Urbach in the region of Hanover, says, in his book, *Protestant or Catholic* (Hildesheim, Franz Borgmeyer, 1881):

> What people call Jesuitism is inseparable from the concept of perfidiousness and immorality, from the justification of every means in order that this party may gain or may assure control over the world. This principle, commonly summarized in the phrase 'the end justifies the means,' is ascribed to the Society of Jesus. But that phrase, found on everyone's lips, which supposedly has been culled from 'Jesuitical morality,' can, with the help of a totally inconspicuous alteration of words, bring about quite the opposite of what this 'Jesuitical morality' is said to teach.

> This "Jesuitical morality" actually says that the *media*, that is to say, those things that lie in the middle, between good and evil, the so-called *adiaphora* (i.e., things, works, etc. that are not in and of themselves either good nor evil) may be justified through the end for which one uses them. The Apostle says the same when he admonishes the Christian that everything that he does, even eating and drinking, be done in the name of Jesus for the glory of God. 'The glory of God' is the motto of the Society of Jesus. I myself was also bogged down in the past by the prejudice that 'Jesuit' and 'the epitome of all wickedness' were quite identical concepts. Since then, thank God, I have been fundamentally cured of this error through the study of the pertinent issues.

Whoever else wishes to be convinced of the groundlessness of the accusation that the Jesuits pay homage to the infamous theory of expediency should actually read their moral theological writings. Admittedly, one needs beforehand some previous knowledge, especially a rigorous knowledge of Latin, in which the majority of these writings are composed. If you want to examine them yourself, you will discover the falsity of this ignominious defamation from the very beginning of their moral theologies in the *Treatise on Human Action* (*In actibus humanis*) in the passage in which the requirements of a morally good action are discussed (Gurn, *Theol. Mor.* 1, n. 21 seq; Lehmkuhl, *Theol. Mor.* 1, n. 28 seq.).

Here all of the well-known moral theologians of the Society of Jesus, unanimously following St. Thomas Aquinas, teach that the moral goodness of an act is dependent upon the convergence of three elements. It must be good not merely with respect to the purpose, but also according to the object and the circumstances involved. If one of these elements is missing, the act will be bad. For: *Bonum ex integra causa, malum ex quocumque defectu* [an action is good when it is good in every respect; an action is wrong when it is wrong in every respect]. Whoever is in the position generally to grasp what is said in these words will have to admit that through them the bad principle of the end justifying the means is totally excluded.

If phrases are found in Jesuit as well as in other moral theologians such as "to whom the end is permitted, to him the means to the end are also allowed," and so forth, they are to be understood in this manner. It is manifest from the context and even expressly highlighted by some Jesuits that it is *means* that are in themselves "indifferent" (*ex objecto et circumstantiis*) that are permitted; the means that Evers calls *adiaphora* in the passage cited above. Means that are bad in and of themselves are from the outset already excluded, due to what we learn from the preceding discussion of morality.

You mention in your letter the "persuasive arguments" that the Hildesheim councilor, Götting, brought up in January of

1883 in the Prussian Chamber of Deputies against "Jesuitism";
arguments that he "victoriously defended" afterwards in a
brochure that he published with Behr in Berlin against one of
his critics. This brochure "by chance fell into your hands" and
made an "indelible impression" upon you.

You are, however, so honest, that you confess that you
admittedly have not read the *Critique of Götting's Address* by
"Ma." in the *Niederrheinische Volkszeitung* (n. 1114-117, 1883)
to which Götting's brochure constituted the "answer." Just
as little have you consulted the *Moral Work* of Father Gurn,
upon which the Hildesheim councilor based his accusation.
Now, as you say, you find that this was "a shortcoming." That
is very true. Perhaps you feel the need belatedly to remedy that
shortcoming?

In this case, I also recommend to you for the further
completion of your studies "Ma.'s" response to the councilor in
his brochure, *Götting and the Moral Theory of Gurn* (Crefeld,
Klein'ische Buchhandlung). It was precisely this brochure that
contributed not a little to the elimination of my own prejudice
against "Jesuitism," and was simultaneously helpful to my
more sound introduction to an understanding of true "Jesuit
morality"; or, more correctly, to the morality of the Catholic
Church, which Protestants find in no way easy to grasp. He
proves here, in an impressive way, that Götting errs on all counts
of his indictment; that he speaks with the greatest injustice of
"Gurn's shameful and villainous morality"; that he mouths
obvious untruths; and that his efforts are nothing more than
plagiarisms from scandalous brochures, in particular from a
brochure of the preacher Spiegel of the Protestant Association.

Furthermore, Götting was not the first German
parliamentarian who has tried to win his knightly spurs in
the Culture Wars through the disparagement of Gurn and
the Jesuits. Even a baptized Catholic deputy, Windthorst—
be it understood, the National Liberal Windthorst from
Bielefeld, and not the leader of the Catholic Centre Party—lent
highly dramatic expression to his "indignation" over Gurn's

"abominable book" in the German Reichstag on May 15, 1872. (He spoke, in the process, exactly like my friend D., perhaps in unconscious reminiscence, of "this new, foolish dogma of Papal Infallibility").

If it were true that the Jesuits taught such shameful moral principles as they are outrageously accused of doing, how would it then be possible that these principles are not frequently confirmed by their personal lives? Could men with immoral principles be personally moral? Yet even their opponents do not dare to question the private life of the Jesuits. Yes, not a few of them praise their lives. Even that National Liberal Windthorst recognized in his fiery address that the Jesuits led honorable moral lives. Their moral conduct has everywhere and at all times been so irreproachable that it aroused wonder earlier, even among Catholics. Here and there a fairy tale emerged, claiming that they were in possession of an herb that made them immune from temptations, in particular that of dishonesty. The Emperor Ferdinand, upon hearing of this, asked his Jesuit confessor whether there were any truth in it. The latter answered, smiling: "Well, certainly!" "And in what exactly does the magic consist?" the Emperor asked. "The herb," the Jesuit responded, "is called the fear of God."

This is enough for today. My beloved wife, in order to prevent me from writing past midnight, has given me so little oil for my lamp that the light is now about to go out right under my nose. Wives are like that—full of "Jesuitical tricks"! I had still so much *in petto*, but will now have to put you off until next week.

Good night! Your H.

~Chapter 5~
Black Robes and Black Legends

Dear D.!

I know from personal experience just how deeply the prejudice against the Jesuits is rooted in the Protestant mind. I myself once vent my wrath on these "fanatics, skulking about in the dark" in filthy caricatures and still more filthy rhymes. In doing so, I was admittedly, just like other Jesuit-killers, completely uninfluenced by knowledge of individual persons and knowledge of the facts. I had as of then never seen a Jesuit or read one of their books. Why would I anyway? Parents, teachers, preachers had sufficiently informed me about them. Even as a boy I had already zealously read *The Arbor* and similarly instructive pages, alongside a whole heap of even more instructive novels, and from these I had got to know those crafty hypocrites and schemers.

I was also taught sayings such as "test everything and keep the best," but it never came into my head that I should take such wisdom seriously with respect to Catholic matters and even the Jesuits as well. Who could have told me then that I would not detest the Jesuits right up until my death, and that, in fact, I would even learn to honor and love them! Of course not overnight, but slowly, on a long, laborious path filled with thorns. I investigated their writings themselves, not one or a few, but rather many. I came to know some of them personally, and what pearls of Christian wisdom, what endearing, noble men, true disciples of Jesus I found among them!

But it is now as clear to me as the light of day why precisely these men have been so particularly hated, vilified, defamed and persecuted. The words of Jesus themselves would have had not to be words of eternal truth if it had been otherwise! Next to their Christian names, they bear the name of Jesus in a more special way, battling and suffering afflictions in the frontlines on account of His name. They are true knights of the Spirit, luminous in the defense of authentic Christian actions, fearful through their sword of comprehensive and rigorous erudition!

By the way, there are also Protestants whom the Society of Jesus has compelled to appreciate them. They are admittedly only such Protestants who in some way and in some measure have become aware of their true nature and impact. After describing the emergence and the spread of the Jesuit schools in the second half of the sixteenth century, the Berlin Professor Friedrich Paulsen, in his *History of Scholarly Instruction in German Schools and Universities Since the End of the Middle Ages*, comments on the Jesuits themselves as follows:

> Wherein lay the secret of the strength of these men? Was it in the fact that they, as Raumer's verdict rings out, were 'malicious men'? Because they, more cleverly and indiscriminately than all others, exploited both the credulity of the masses as well as the political perplexity and helplessness of rulers in opposing the Revolution? That seems to me to put more confidence in the strength of falsehood than this can really orchestrate. An old saying has it that the strongest man is he who overcomes himself. Perhaps that saying does not mean merely that the greatest strength is required to overcome oneself, but also that the greatest impact comes from someone who has done so. I indeed believe that there has never been a society of men that has advanced more continuously in the taming of the natural drives of its members, the repressing of their individual appetites, than that of the Jesuits.

Macaulay affirms: "No religious community could account for a string of such diverse men of excellence; none has extended its undertakings over such a wide area…These have expanded this to lands to whose exploration neither commercial avarice nor scientific curiosity had ever driven a foreigner" (*History of England*, Stuttgart, 1850, III, 58). Ranke, at the end of a short presentation of the Jesuit missions and their success, also proclaims in awe: "An immeasurable, global activity! Nevertheless, everywhere fresh and indefatigable on this unlimited stage!" (*History of the Popes*, II, 496).

The civilizing activity of the Jesuits in America has been truly admirable from the outset. Educated Protestants, here and there, admit their achievements in Paraguay. It was in Paraguay, as the Protestant church historian Kurtz says, where the savages who had been converted lived, happily and contentedly, in a liberally organized political system, "as children would have done, guided by a tender mother's hand, under the mild patriarchal supervision of the Jesuits for the long term of one hundred forty years (1610-1750). Even Voltaire thinks that their work here "was a triumph of humanitarianism."

The Protestant Dr. Bernhard Förster, who himself lived long years in Paraguay, writes in one of his works appearing in the 1880s (*German Colonials in the Upper La Plata Region, with Special Consideration of Paraguay*): "The Jesuits continued, in an awesome way, the educational and assimilation process of the Guarani population which had been given to them from the beginning of the seventeenth century in the beautiful areas on both sides of the Upper Parana as far as the Tebicuary, and on both sides of the Upper Uruguay; districts that still today bear the name of "the missions" and partly belong to Paraguay, partly to Argentina and partly to Brazil. There can be no doubt that the Jesuits sacrificed themselves here, with wise understanding for the nature of childlike peoples, and acted thoroughly beneficially on their behalf. Judge their expulsions in Europe as one may, the extension of this prohibition to the land of their almost two hundred year-long activity, successful and in no way finished, was not only an act of brutal barbarism but also of shortsighted folly."

Less known in Europe is the enormous share the Jesuits had in the exploration and Christianizing of North America. They were culture warriors in the most noble sense of that term. The Protestant poet and historian Washington Irving says:

"The Catholics priests came before the merchants and soldiers themselves; from sea to sea, from river to river, the Jesuits hurried restlessly forward and expended an energy that no other Christians have ever shown" (Knickerbocker, June, 1838). Alex von Humboldt describes the Jesuits as model missionaries when he writes:

> Fast progress can be made as soon as one operates according to the procedure of the Jesuits, giving extraordinary support to the most remote missions and placing missionaries who are the most courageous, the most reasonable, and the most skilled in Indian languages in the most outlying stations. These missionaries are everywhere the first on the spot in South as well as in North America. (*Journeys in the Equatorial Regions*, Stuttgart, 1862, VI, 56f.)

Already two hundred years before the United States made its appearance in history, they were dedicating their work and lives, goods and blood, to the exploration and civilizing of the land that now forms part of its territory. The books of Bancroft and Parkman, of Longfellow and Irving, give witness to their heroic, groundbreaking activity.Said our greatest historian, the Protestant George Bancroft, "when did a Jesuit missionary ever seek to save his own life so long as he believed a soul was in danger? The names of Fathers Jogues, Bréboeuf, Hennepin, Marquette, Carroll (the first Bishop of the United States), Francisco Kino, de Smet and many others will always stand out in every true cultural history of North America, continuously will be recorded as being among the best." T h e Protestant Dr. G.A. Zimmerman writes,

> Seldom in history have men joyful in their faith taken upon themselves such a manifold activity in all the difficulties, dangers and hardships of the wilderness with such zeal and seriousness as the Canadian Jesuits Le Jeune, Bréboeuf, Jogues and many others. The energy, persistency and finesse of these men were downright miraculous,

and one must be filled with admiration when reading the moving accounts of the struggles that these "Romans of the New World" and their protégés, the Hurons, had to fight against their deadly enemies, the Iroquois; of their martyrs' deaths and the ferocious treatment on the part of these enemies that preceded them." They were "men who with fervid enthusiasm for the conversion of an entire continent happily tolerated frost and heat, privation and death." (*Four Hundred Years of American History*, Milwaukee, 1893, pp. 125-12 6).

The Jesuits are slandered as enemies of popular freedom and especially as the worst enemies of religious tolerance. But the counselors of those Maryland Catholics who first planted the banner of religious freedom in our land were the Jesuits, and their sincere attachment to our republican institutions has never been put into question by any of their activities here. Never has any Jesuit committed any act of treason or disloyalty in the United States. The Jesuits displayed a self-sacrificing activity in the Civil War on the battlefields and in the hospitals, just like their brethren in the Franco-German War of 1870-1871. And while they were being vilified in the German Parliament, they found panegyrists in the Congress of the United States, even on the part of Protestant representatives. Hence, among others, the Missourian [George] Vest, one of the most important of the members of the United States Senate, has repeatedly given eloquent witness to their beneficial activity as culture bearers among the Indians, and indeed on the grounds of his own personal observation.

Professor Gerhard Bergrath vom Rath of Bonn, in his work *Studies and Perceptions* (Heidelberg, Karl Winter, 1885), has interesting notes on the beneficial activity of the old Jesuits in Mexico and especially in contemporary Arizona, which parallel those in Paraguay in their length of time. Towards the end of the sixteenth century the Spanish conquerors subjugated the whole west coast of North America, along with wide strips of the hinterland, Arizona among them.

Next to the deeds of the conquerors, marked by avarice, thirst for fame, and yes, first and foremost, through cruelty, the charity and the self-sacrifice of many priests who brought the Indians Christianity, a higher civilized mode of behavior, and the arts of peace arose to distinguish themselves. Much misjudged and much slandered, they were the sublime models of Christian life and activity even where their devotion was not crowned with success. Men with German names were also among these true priests and men of charity, such as the great benefactor of the Mexican Indians, Pedro de Gante, 'a native of the city of Yguen (Ypern?) in the county of Flanders.' The Emperor Charles V sent this noble man to Mexico, where he worked for almost fifty years, to the great blessing of the population. He preached in the Mexican language and instructed the Indians, particularly in music and in the mechanical arts. On his request, the Empress sent six matrons for the education of Indian maidens in female handicrafts. He converted innumerable souls and consecrated over one hundred churches.

A priest in the spirit of Gante, who died in 1687, was Francis Kino, S.J., the great missionary of Arizona (a German, Kühn). Julius Fröbel, who travelled through Arizona in 1853, reports: "I cannot easily remember a greater surprise than that of the sight of the premises of the old and renowned Mission of San Xavier del Bac (founded by Kühn and Salvatieraz in 1687), which stood there as a monument to the great effectiveness and energy of the old Catholic missionaries, here in a natural environment of sublime but unpretentious grandeur. Next to the stately Church stand the low earth huts of the few still living Pima, who are proud to be Christians. They are good-natured, quiet, honest men of a mild character and a strict discipline, who, for a long time, have been lacking secular instruction." When Father Kühn closed his eyes after a quarter of a century of self-sacrificing and successful work, he left behind eight flourishing missions. Vom Rath describes still further (p. 69):

These missions possessed herds of cattle, sheep, and horses; large areas were converted into farmlands and produced good harvests; extensive mining for silver was conducted. The life in the missions was that of a large Christian family. The Indians went to Church in the mornings for prayer and early Mass. A bell then called the workers to the square in whose middle the Church stood. Here, the priests assigned to each of them his work, watched over and instructed the people during the day, either themselves or through trustworthy Mexicans who were put in charge of the job. At sunset, the workers returned home to their dwellings, which lay round about the square. A priest, standing in the middle of the square, said the evening prayer in their native language. Indians who stood between the priest and the huts repeated the words loudly, and in this way that prayer penetrated into all the dwellings, in which every father then spoke them before the other family members. Moreover, the Indians were not only trained in prayer and field work, but also made some progress in reading and writing; an alphabet in the Pima Language was prepared.

The abolition of the Society of Jesus in 1767 delivered a severe blow to the missions. The Fathers had to quit the sites of an eighty-year activity. Their successors, the Franciscans, equally left nothing lacking in either energy or self-sacrifice, but soon the Apaches, who were not mentioned in the earlier reports, appeared on the scene as irreconcilable enemies of the Whites and of all of those tribes who were allied with them. The defection of Mexico from the Spanish Motherland brought death to the missions, since the government left them first defenseless, and then, in 1827, abolished them. Robbed of protection against the attacks of the Apaches, the missions quickly fell to their destiny, and the fruits of one hundred forty years of charitable work were lost.

I almost fear that I have kept you focused on this subject longer than you might like. But the man whose heart is full cannot remain quiet. And it always "warms" my heart when I think how even well-meaning Protestants in our beloved Germany have been able to ally themselves with dishonest "liberal" rabble, in order to expel the Jesuits and keep them out, and when I think that among these are even some who stand close to me through friendship and blood relationship.

What a disastrous blindness! You all fear for Protestantism because of the Jesuits. And yet the Prussian General and Minister, Theodor H.R. von Rochow, although a Protestant through and through, has said: "The Jesuits are less dangerous to Protestantism than their own theologians." And this is true, if one understands as Protestantism whatever exists in Protestant circles that is still Christian. If you were not completely blinded, it would greatly perplex you that the main voices in the battle against the Jesuits are precisely those "liberals," theologians and others, who are the least interested in Christ. Even a Heinrich Heine, who shares their position with respect to Christ, puts you to shame. "Poor Fathers of the Society of Jesus," he exclaims; "you are the bogeymen and the scapegoats of the Liberal Party. As far I am concerned, I could never join in in the clamor of my comrades, who always fall into a rage at the mention of the name of Loyola, like bulls before those waving a red cloth at them."

The Jesuits are said to be "men without a country." Oh, ignominious slander! Travel abroad and really learn of these men whom you—many of you even after a "thankful" Fatherland honored them with the Iron Cross—have driven from their hearth and home. Come to know them! I have never found so often such a hardcore German attitude as among these Jesuits driven from Germany to live abroad. The song that one of them—Father Johann V. Diehl (*Poems*, Freiburg, Herder)— sang in foreign climes of "The German Heart" is still alive today among his German brethren in exile:

> A German heart is consecrated ground,
> From it, fidelity shoots up towards heaven;
> It is a blessed chamber,
> Like unto that of precious metal;

A sea in which many a pearl rests
Dropped by God into the tide;
A springtime font that rings resoundingly,
That sings to the Lord songs of praise;
It is a noble lustrous stone,
So hard, so glowing, and so pure,
And in a word: In joy and pain,
It is the profound German heart;
That so closely binds itself to God,
So artlessly greets each enemy,
So heatedly glows with all things exalted;
And with such abhorrence flees all things base;
That settles, steadfastly chained,
To its beloved German Fatherland.

That golden German heart from which this song poured forth beat its last, before its time, like so many others, on the foreign soil to which a brutal government, moved by human folly and diabolical evil, had expelled it.

Your H.

~Chapter 6~

A Lutheran Defense
of the Society of Jesus

Dear D.,

I could have spared myself the previous letter if I had waited a few days more. Afterwards, an article about the Jesuits appearing in the Protestant *Landeszeitung* of Reuss of the Elder Line {a German State} and published in the Lutheran *Hessischen Blättern* came into to my hands. A Lutheran wrote this article, and such an impartial appreciation of the Society of Jesus from the pen of a Lutheran has honestly never come before my eyes. Although I have now expressed myself rather thoroughly regarding this subject, nevertheless I think that an excerpt from this remarkable essay perhaps would still be welcome.

As you know, at the time when the essay appeared, we were dealing with the question of whether the German Federal Council would or would not agree to the decision of the Reichstag to abrogate the Jesuit Law. The author of the very comprehensive and thoroughgoing essay now under discussion approved that proposal fully and resolutely. To begin with, out of a "sense of justice," he judged that law to be:

[A] law that was an exceptional measure called into being against the Jesuits, rebuking a number of German citizens of the country to which they belonged by their birth and their profession, without there being anyone in a position to make an accusation against them or even having made an attempt to provide a proof of the existence of an unpatriotic sense or enmity to the country on the part of those being penalized.

Even generally known facts spoke in favor of those who were banished. Members of the Society of Jesus distinguished themselves to the highest degree in the wars between 1866 and 1871. The Emperor Wilhelm I expressed his imperial thanks to them in a public statement honoring them on May 21, 1871. They returned home after the French War, decorated with a war medallion. As the war reports indicated, these men had exposed themselves to every danger on the battlefield and in the field hospitals in order to care for the wounded, physically, and also to be able to administer words of consolation to their souls.

Also of great significance with respect to this point was the brilliant witness given the Society in the General Report of the Central Authority of the Johannite-Maltese Society in Rhineland Westphalia. These were the same Jesuits who soon afterwards would be identified as enemies of the Empire and whose expulsion from the Fatherland would be considered a simple patriotic duty; and this, as though to document that there certainly lies a world of difference between national rhetorical cant and deeds produced by love of country.

After a cutting and damning judgment with respect to the whole "Culture War"; "that abominable episode, that casts an irremovable shame upon the history of our German Fatherland," one finds in this article an appeal to the Protestant "sense of truth," as well as a pitiless exposure of certain lying publications that have been disseminated to thwart the revocation of the Jesuit Law.

The author then moves on to an illumination of the question of wherein the "actual cause" of the fear of the Jesuits lies. At this point, that part of this excellent essay shapes up as a wholehearted defense of the Society of Jesus. To begin with, he cites on their behalf the witness of the Protestant Professor Paulsen whom I have already mentioned. Following this, he says:

> The famous Johannes von Müller, also a Protestant, expressed himself in his *World History* in the same way in his own day: 'The plan of the Society of Jesus was simple, meaningful and innocent. This Society merits comparison with the great institutions of the lawgivers of the Ancient World. It gave to its members an extraordinary field of

activity and such a precise standard of obedience that the whole Society resembled a healthy body ruled by a firm and steady soul. Since the time of Pythagoras there has been no institute in history that has simultaneously given laws to barbarous as well as half and also extremely refined peoples with such great success. Indeed, they were all things to all people.'

Even Prince Bismarck, whose statements on this subject have always admittedly been only of secondary significance for us, since he, as an open practitioner of Realpolitik, has never allowed himself to be guided by principles, and in fact could not allow himself to be so guided, has invariably understood how to adapt his public role to whatever his particular momentary political goals might be. Consequently, in the period of the Culture Wars, he represented what one was generally accustomed to think regarding the Jesuits. But this great enemy of the Jesuits, after the political constellation had in the meantime considerably changed, was heard to speak the following words in the Reichstag sitting of November 28, 1885, with respect to their missionary activity in the German Protectorates in Africa: 'The Society is more knowledgeable, more tolerant, more clever than many others. The Jesuits are no mere observers—I speak with esteem of them—they are a force, a power to which no one can deny his recognition.'

The tightly knit unity of the Roman Catholic Church, her well-organized and authoritative insertion of the individual lives of believers into her system, and the laws of the finely-structured whole displays itself in the Society of Jesus in a superlatively enhanced manner. We believe that it is here that the specific character of this institution is most succinctly expressed. This enormous mass of self-sacrifice of personal wills, this complete opening of the individual personality to that ecclesiastical whole into which it knows itself to be incorporated, does have its unmistakable dangers; this cannot be denied. We can comprehend that such a conception of the nature of the Church and the relationship of the members to the whole can, under circumstances, place most painful weights upon the consciences of individuals. On the other hand, it also cannot be denied that the idea as such, apart from the possibility of the abusive forms this may take, corresponds to the Scriptural concept of the Church, and that a realization of this that is drawn from the actual life of the Faith can be an incalculable boon. The same double-sided perception can be made in the military realm.

Turning to the Protestant camp—we now do indeed turn thence—Protestants should show themselves ready to learn from the Roman Church in general and from the Jesuits in particular. In fact, it could not harm us, but rather, very much be of use. In fact, what is it that we see everywhere we turn our glance when looking to evangelical regions? Distraction and perplexity; a most frivolous subjectivism, which, wrapping itself under the cover of "independent research," scarcely stops before the most fundamental articles of the Christian Faith, the more dangerously and destructively doing its work precisely the more it clothes itself in the vestments of a falsely understood 'evangelical freedom.' We find everywhere an astonishing lack of consciousness of that which has been ordained for the continued existence of the Church and which is necessary for the propagation of ecclesiastical life and its stable regulation, the disregard of which can have as its consequence only a crippling of the general and the individual life of the Faith, leading to its eventual destruction. Moreover, we find a thousand other things whose presence insightful Protestants most deeply lament, without their being in a position to indicate means and ways of introducing better conditions.

Our special interest in confronting testimonials regarding the nature and significance of the Society of Jesus on the one hand with these plaintive remarks on evangelical conditions on the other is sufficiently obvious. On the grounds of this comparison we would like to try to indicate the reasons why the Society of Jesus, which is numerically so insignificant, is nevertheless once again so much feared today by Evangelicals in a totally unique way, and why they risk everything to thwart that abrogation of the Jesuit Law which is under consideration; an abrogation that one hears is in no way looked upon unsympathetically by the reigning Emperor and his Chancellor.

As scatterbrained as those ecclesiastical and political parties from whose midst such terrifying anti-Jesuit publications are promoted seem to be, they must necessarily fear men who ecclesiastically and politically know exactly what they want. Ecclesiastical freedom and impotence have at all times been frightened of ecclesiastical consistency and energy. Having said this, we can now indicate where it is that we can find the key to the solution of the mysterious riddle of the just as mysterious fear of the Jesuits.

Bebel, on June 17th, 1872 and Liebknecht, on January 11th, 1883 {the two main leaders of the German Social Democratic Party}, both at that time arguably proceeding from a somewhat different point of view than they would today, made the declaration in the German Reichstag that that they 'stood against the Jesuits in the most hostile way,' and that their party's effort 'was aimed at an extirpation of the Jesuits' because international Social Democracy feared that these representatives of authority in both State and Church might once again let themselves be employed against the Social Democrats. It seems that those in the circles of the Evangelical Church indicated above are gripped by the same concern: namely, that these 'dexterous spiritual gentlemen' might once again deliver and this time complete the *coup de grace* against the frailty and feebleness of the Evangelical Church on her own territory.

For our part, we have not the slightest objection to the self-conscious determination of Jesuitism; we do not in the least censure this. On the contrary, we highly honor the firm character of the Jesuits; we treasure their energetic zeal for the strengthening of their own Church, for her spread and her service in every respect in those ecclesiastical communities from which we know ourselves to be divorced in many matters, be they dogmatic or otherwise.

We stand in the greatest degree of hostility only to two developments: 1) ecclesiastical indifferentism, whether this be found on either the Lutheran or the Catholic side, or that of any other Church's terrain as well, and, 2) something that is once again linked together only due to a highly lamentable weakness; that peculiar zeal (if such a word may properly be used here) that believes that one should appeal to the help of the state authorities and its police organs in support of one's own ecclesiastical position, even to the disadvantage of other church communities. Windthorst is fully correct here when he repeats and determinedly asserts that the ecclesiastical differences of the two largest communities, the Roman and the Evangelical Church, can only be brought to a halt by means of a peaceful discussion. This seems to us to be not only a requirement for ecclesiastical propriety, but a claim that (and we assert this here calmly against even that curious 'Christian worldview' of a certain conservative circle, especially in Prussia) fits together also with the innermost nature and essence of the Christian Church.

We might now conclude. However, we would like for several moments more to touch upon one further aspect of the present question that seems to us cannot be left out or neglected. That is the fact that the general impression of the Society of Jesus and its danger are for the most part erroneous; it arises in many cases from a mistaken fantasy, often from caricatures that lack all historical foundation.

Indeed, even the committedly "modern" Berlin weekly, Schorer's *Familienblatt* (1887, n. 18), which appears under a Protestant publisher and editor, writes the following regarding the Society: 'Public opinion creates for itself a nightmarish caricature of the Jesuits and their institutions. It cannot completely be reproached for doing so, for the history books from which the modern world draws its knowledge of the Society of Jesus have described it in this way and in no other. But everything that the historians and novelist-poets have recounted of the most calculating cleverness, of the Mephistophelian arts and crimes and similar deeds of the Jesuits, are the hideous lies and soap bubbles of outright fantasies or of evil hearts. The Society of Jesus is the model order, for it has never needed a reform. Its powerful position and its successes are the fruit of that wondrous organization that reveals it to be the best institute that has ever been created by wise men. In our day, where the Jesuits once again desire entry into the German Empire, it would be timely and good for us to draft a true picture of them.'

These statements are accompanied by the declarations of other personalities who are equally on their side, but whose judgment is nevertheless otherwise commonly held by the most free thinking men of our century to be of the most profound significance. We cite the English Chancellor Bacon, the Protestant historian Macaulay, the Frenchmen Montesquieu and Rousseau, and, from Germany, men like Leibnitz, Lessing, Herder, Wieland and Goethe. The extremely freethinking Prussian King Frederick the Great, who was more than too much influenced by Voltaire, was also, as is generally well known, the most decisive defender of the Jesuits.

However bitter a pill that they may constitute for

certain conservative circles, particularly in Prussia, We cannot suppress two further judgments. Let us first call up a dictum of Heinrich Heine, found in the first volume of his *Miscellanies* (Hamburg, 1834, p.108). {Here follows the citation already mentioned by H.}. Still more harsh, if possible, is the passage that the former Protestant Professor Kern of Göttingen wrote to the enraged enemies of the Jesuits in 1824: 'Among non-Catholics, namely, from among the Protestants, the greatest minds or the noblest hearts have, from the very beginning, declared themselves to be favorable to the Catholics or to the Jesuits as soon as they became properly familiarized with their nature and when no other more intimate private interest held them back from the expression of their opinion...(and there now follows a rather lengthy list of the most significant men already cited above)...Conversely, however, it is precisely the narrowest minds or the most ignoble hearts, the most sinister party members, who always strike out most furiously against the Catholics and the Jesuits from among us Protestants.'

Incidentally, perhaps no rational Protestant dares to dispute the laudable and sterling quality of the scholarliness of the Society of Jesus. After all, even the famous Professor Benschlag, a firm enemy of the Jesuits, found himself obliged in his *Deutsch Evangelische Blättern* (March, 1891) to return the following verdict: 'The special disciplines of the Jesuits extend almost through the entire domain of human knowledge, and it would be unjust to deny to them the admission that a great number of them have achieved splendid things therein.'

Thus defends the Jesuits, my dear D., a man who, as he himself says, "is devoted to the teachings of the Evangelical-Lutheran Church with all his heart."

Your H.

~Chapter 7~
Saved by Faith Alone

Dear D.,

So you have forgotten to touch upon "a major point of the controversy" and now seek to make up for that failure. A sentence in my last letter "struck you greatly"—the fact that I, as a Catholic, wrote: "We only expect grace and eternal salvation from God on account of the merit of Christ." You think that this is actually "a totally evangelical phrase." After all, according to Catholic teaching, eternal salvation is dependent upon good works.

My dear D., the Catholic teaching on justification is unfortunately just as misunderstood and disfigured on the part of Protestants as practically everything else; and one Protestant then thoughtlessly repeats to others all of this absurd stuff from generation to generation.

Now we Catholics do not believe that anyone can, through his own works, independent from the merits and the suffering of Jesus Christ and His grace, win his salvation or obtain satisfaction for his sins or gain any merit whatsoever. On the contrary, we believe that justification is a grace earned through Jesus Christ, which will be bestowed on us completely without our merit. The Bible, which is held in honor as Holy Writ among Catholics far more than it is among you, repeats this truth in many passages. "You are justified without merit," says Paul in his *Epistle to the Romans*, in which he generally wants to prove that everyone, Jews and Gentiles, are called to the Faith without their merit. "It happens through grace," he concludes, "and therefore not from works." As a result, the Church has not only never taught the doctrine that sinners can justify themselves due to their own strength, or even *begin* the work of justification in the slightest, but in battling against the Pelagians and semi-Pelagians, has also expressly and solemnly condemned it.

However, just as it is essential that God, in order to justify men (to make them righteous) anticipates this effort with His grace, it is also vital that the awakened sinner—who has again lost the cloth of righteousness that he obtained through the grace of Baptism—cooperate with this help in his disposition and with his deeds. Heaven gives us the grace without our assistance; it practically lays this treasure at our door, but it does not compel us; we can take it or we can leave it lying there. "*Fecit nescientem, justificat volentem,*" as St. Augustine says: "He who created you without yourself does not justify you without yourself"; that is to say, without your will. In the story of the cure of the man with the palsy (John 5:2ff), Jesus does not heal the sick man without further ado, but rather first asks him: "Do you wish to be made whole?" Only after his affirmative answer does he restore his health. Therefore, an act of will of the sick man is added to the grace of the Redeemer. Here you have the Catholic conception of cooperation in a nutshell.

In no way is the cooperation of the sinner with divine grace—i.e., his good works—the reason for our justification according to Catholic doctrine. Rather, the beginning of salvation, the foundation and root of justification lies, according to this doctrine, in Faith. The Council of Trent expressly teaches this. However, good works are the fruits of justification. Bred from our freedom, these works are certainly ours and do earn reward. Brought forth by the grace which enlivens our wills, they are gifts of God of which we never make use for our own particular profit, and of which we are not permitted in the least to feel any pride.

For what would we have been able to do without the help of God? "Without me, you can do nothing" (John 15:5), the Divine Master said, and the Apostle Paul notes: "No one can say: Lord Jesus, except through the Holy Spirit" (1 Corinthians, 12:13). St. Augustine cries out,

> Righteous souls, multiply your good works, for 'a good tree brings forth good fruit' (Matthew 7:17), and, 'a tree that brings forth no good fruits is torn up and thrown into

the fire' (Matthew 3:10) ...While you practice these pious works, however, strain yourselves doubly to be humble, so that haughtiness does not poison your virtue and accelerate your fall. 'Watch and pray,' as you have been instructed, for 'the spirit is willing but the flesh is weak' (Matthew 26:4). Be thankful to God; therein lies righteousness; be strict with yourselves, therein also lies righteousness; do not judge your brother, for 'he who stands or falls, stands or falls before his Master' (Romans 14:4); and 'when you have done all those things which have been commanded you, say, we are useless servants.' (Luke 17:10)

Perhaps you might say, 'not so useless', if only the *Epistle to the Romans* did not expressly tell us: "For we think that a man can be righteous through Faith alone without the works of the Law." Yes, "if"! But have you ever once looked at the passage in the original text and in its context? First of all, there is no trace of the word "alone." Luther added this word in his translation so as to make his new teaching on justification more plausible than it could have been "as written." Take the unadulterated text and the passage in context with the rest of the *Epistle* and they will not offer you the slightest difficulty. What is at stake here is the contrast between the Christian Faith and the "works of the Law"; that is to say, the Jewish ceremonial Law, not "good works" in the Catholic sense. These latter possess an inner justification and have the Faith—the true, living, Faith stimulated through love to be fruitful—as a precondition; the other does not.

Now Luther also denied that the Faith had to be a Faith stimulated by love (*fidex formata*) in order to achieve eternal salvation. But since Scripture was not sufficient to prove this, he called for help upon the faculty of reason that was otherwise so often decried by him:

> If a man hears that he should believe in Christ, and that although such a Faith cannot help or be of use to him, because it is love, when coming into the picture, that gives to this Faith its power, making it capable of working for

men's righteousness in a way that can never fail, then the following can happen. He can lose the Faith, doubt, and thus come to think that if his *faith* in love does not make him righteous, then *Faith* is certainly unprofitable and actually amounts to nothing in itself; that love alone can make a man righteous. If Faith does not have love to give to it its correct form, making it capable of his becoming righteous, this means that Faith has no significance. If, however, Faith is nothing, how can it then make one righteous?

I cannot better illustrate the spurious beauty of this logic than with the words of the Freiherr von Hammerstein, the convert already mentioned above, who writes: "Similarly we could prove that wood does not burn. To wit: If wood does not burn without fire, it is certainly unprofitable and worth nothing, and fire alone can burn; if no fire is laid upon the wood in order to give it its correct form, that is to say, to inflame it, than wood is nothing. If, however, it is nothing, how then can it burn?" (*Memoirs*, 48, 49).

The German-American convert, Hermann Baumstark, formerly a Lutheran preacher and professor in the seminary in St. Louis, a man who ended up in the Catholic Church almost simultaneously with his brother, Reinhold Baumstark, an attorney in Baden—but through a completely different and more reliable path—writes:

> I came to understand the teaching on justification in the following manner. I compared the wording of both passages which express the apparent contradiction between Paul and James most sharply (Romans 3:28): 'And so we maintain that man is justified through Faith without the works of the Law'; and James 2:24: 'You see therefore that man is justified through works and not through Faith alone.' The artificial attempt that is made on the part of Protestants to remove this apparent contradiction between Paul and James never satisfied me; this was a difficulty to

which I always had to confess that I had not yet found the correct solution.

"Now I confronted this once more in all its starkness with the firm desire to find a simple, uncontrived solution to it, thinking that God would allow someone who was searching honestly for the truth to discover this very point which was so important and decisive for the salvation of men. At first glance, the comparison of both passages made the contradiction appear just as insoluble as ever, for the one seemed pretty much to deny with the same words what the other one affirmed. But the difference between the both of them that now immediately became clear to me lay in the words "of the Law" with which Paul indicated the works that he was identifying, while this expression was missing in James. The new, illuminating thought then arose in my mind that the true solution to the difficulty must lie in the fact that Paul meant another kind of work than that found in James, and that this in no way excluded that which was identified by the latter. (*Unsere Wege zur Katholischen Kirche*, Reinhold and Hermann Baumstark, Freiburg, Herder, 1870)

"Work based," "works-righteousness!" How those words pour forth from the mouth of the Protestant who is prejudiced against Rome whenever he comes to speak of this theme. He talks himself into a "holy" indignation, because before the eye of the spirit there immediately stands incarnate the repellent figure of the Pharisee in the Temple, who, insisting upon his good works, looks down arrogantly upon the poor publican. This, to him, is the embodiment of the Catholic teaching on justification. What a tragic blindness! As though what Christ Himself compared to a whited sepulcher that was inwardly full of corruption were supposed to be our sense of sanctity!

I want to draw for you a picture of the "works-righteous" Catholic as he really is. When he rises from his resting place in the morning, his first thought is of the Triune God. He renews his confession of his Faith and the confession of his unworthiness before Him. He thanks Him for the new day, consecrates it to Him through his pious intention: he offers up to God anew all of his labors, difficulties, sorrows and joys. And in doing so he invokes God's blessing, for he is deeply aware of his weakness, his inability to live according to God's holy will through his own strength. All for the honor of God, all for God, all with God; that is his total desire.

And he strives throughout the day to hold fast to this disposition and put it into practice, insofar as human weakness makes it possible. For this reason, he frequently directs his gaze above. Finally, he ends his day with this disposition as well. Before the face of God, invoking His assistance, he looks back at the day in order to spot where and how he failed. He confesses and repents in the deepest humility all of his errors in thought, word and deed, asking God for forgiveness and commending himself to His mercy and His protection. He fosters the most sincere good will towards his neighbor, friend and enemy, without concern for their particular Faith. And the more good works that he does, through prayer, fasting, almsgiving, and the like, the less he thinks of himself, and all the greater is his concern for others.

If you want to learn about the Catholic teaching on justification in still more detail, I recommend to you a reading of Johann Adam Möhler's *Symbolik*, which was of yeoman service to me precisely regarding this question, which is as difficult as it is significant.

With a friendly greeting, your H.

~Chapter 8~
The Sacrament of Confession: A Manmade Insult to Jesus Christ

My Dear D.!

So, on to Confession, that "awful auricular Confession!"

This was also a major objection that my good mother brought up against the Catholic Church. Why not confess one's sins to God Himself? And how can one keep them all in mind, since according to God's word itself, the just man falls seven times a day? It constitutes a non-Gospel moral constraint, an invention of priests, and so on and so forth!

In a Lutheran newspaper in America (*Herold und Zeitschrift*, March, 1883) I once read the defense given by an Anglican preacher in Cleveland, Ohio, who had been accused by another Protestant newspaper of a "public passage towards Rome"; among other reasons, because he had introduced his congregation to "auricular confession and absolution." The Lutheran newspaper wrote:

> With respect to the 'auricular confession' introduced by the Rector in Cleveland, the matter does not seem to have been as bad as depicted. Apparently he does this merely at the request of a communicant, while seeking to have a father-confessor's relationship to the members of his congregation. And indeed, every conscientious pastor must also have experienced how such a thing may be considered and misconstrued by malicious men. But if pressure were used to make someone confess and count up his sins, then such an act would indeed be non-evangelical.

> As for what concerns absolution, it is, unfortunately, all too true that it is common to decry this genuinely evangelical act as being Romish and Papist. Absolution is,

however, genuinely evangelical, because it is totally backed by Scripture. If not, what is it that the Lord Jesus intends to say when He gives the key of binding and loosening into the hands of the congregation (!) (Matthew 18:18) or when He assures his disciples (John 20:23) that those 'to whom you remit their sins,' and so forth? For what else is it that St. Paul wishes to say when he writes to the Corinthians (2 Corinthians 2:10): 'And to whom you have pardoned any thing, I also. For, what I have pardoned, if I have pardoned any thing, for your sakes have I done it in the person of Christ,' other than the fact that the preachers [*sic*] of the Gospel absolve in the place of Christ? For this reason every child in our Church is taught that the forgiveness given by the confessor is 'God's forgiveness,' and that one 'must not doubt, but rather firmly believe that his sins are thereby forgiven before God in Heaven.'

Since you yourself have been raised Lutheran, and according to your last letter you still today accept the Lutheran standpoint with respect to the Catholic practice of confession, I will, therefore, take the above statements of a Lutheran newspaper as the starting point for my following analysis.

The above-mentioned passage from Matthew 18:18 says: "Amen I say to you, whatsoever you shall bind upon earth, shall be bound also in heaven; and whatsoever you shall loose upon earth, shall be loosed also in heaven." In John 20:21-23, we read: "Peace be to you. As the Father hath sent me, I also send you. When he had said this, he breathed on them; and he said to them: Receive ye the Holy Ghost. Whose sins you shall forgive, they are forgiven them; and whose sins you shall retain, they are retained." And Christ our Lord Himself affirms this in the most solemn manner; indeed not to "the congregation," but rather to His Apostles. In doing so, He obviously confers upon the Apostles a sublime task: and He equips them for this with the gift of the Holy Spirit. He tells them as plain as day what the task is that awaits them: to loose and to bind, to remit and to retain sins.

Christ the Lord, in doing this, thereby creates a complete judiciary. Just as the earthly judge may not only absolve, but also condemn, so the spiritual judge as well. Both powers are here clearly and explicitly handed over to him, the power to forgive sins and to retain them, to loose and to bind. "Absolution is genuinely evangelical"; indeed this is true; but no less so is the denial of absolution, the power of binding. But how could the spiritual judge know whether he is to loose or to bind, to remit or to retain sins, if he does not exactly know the sins of the penitent who appears before his bench? If absolution is evangelical, then certainly the avowal of sins, confession, is also evangelical.

Nevertheless, Catholic confession is said to be not only not evangelical, but also alien to Christian Antiquity; if not first introduced into the Church through the Fourth Lateran Council, then by Pope Leo I. But this assertion is thoroughly refuted by Tradition and the history of confession since the oldest times. The necessity and divine institution of confession is indirectly attested to by all of those passages of the Fathers which vindicate the truth of the bishops and priests as successors of the Apostles possessing the binding and loosening power or the power of the keys. Calvin himself admits the conclusiveness of this argument, although he completely rejects confession with a feeling of "evangelical" self-importance.

Indeed it is precisely under the assumption that priests can forgive sins that the urgent calls in the writings of the Fathers to make their sins known to priests (*not* to the congregation) and the fact that they were confessed to them are to be explained. In the first century, Clement, the disciple and successor of St Peter, says: "St. Peter taught that we must ourselves reveal our bad thoughts to the priest." (Clement, *Second Epistle to the Corinthians*). In the third century, Origen says: "If we have confessed our sins not only before God, but also before those who can heal our wounds and sins, then our sins will be eradicated" (*Homily 17 in Luc.* 2:35). Already in many of his passages one finds the comparison of the priest with the doctor, and also that of the sinner with the sick man whose wound cannot be healed before he has seen the doctor. St. Basil says: "It is absolutely necessary that sins be made known to those to whom the stewardship of the mysteries has been entrusted" (*Reg. brev.* 228, ed. Maurin, II, 516). Cyprian, Irenaeus, Tertullian, among others, speaks similarly.

From the later Patristic Era the number of reports of Catholic confession and its necessity are downright massive. Cyril of Jerusalem (fourth century) says: "Confess what you have committed in words or works, at night or during the day" (*Cat.* 1, 5). Ambrose (fifth century) writes: "But they say: 'We give reverence to God when we reserve to Him alone the power to forgive sins.' And yet none can cause Him a greater offense so much as those who disregard His commands and place upon Him the duty that has been laid upon them themselves. For since the Lord Jesus Himself said in the Gospel: 'Receive ye the Holy Spirit; whose sins you shall forgive, they are forgiven them; and whose sins you shall retain, they are retained' (John, 20:21-23), who honors Him more? He who hearkens to His commands, or he who goes against them?" (*De poena* lib. 1, c. 2,6). John Chrysostom in 407 admonishes his listeners: 'Do not accuse yourself solely of divorce and such matters, which are well known among men; confess your defamations and evil backbiting…and all such things as well' (*Hom. In St. Matthew*, 41, 42). Jerome explains in 420: "The bishop or the priest, after he has, in accord with his duty, heard the various aspects of the sins, knows who should be bound and who should be loosed" (*Comm. On St. Matthew*, 16:19). Augustine (in the fifth century) writes: 'No one says within himself: 'I do penance secretly, I do it before God.' Did Christ therefore say in vain: 'Whatever you loose on earth will also be loosed in Heaven?' Were the keys given to the Church in vain? Should we thwart the words of the Gospel, the words of Christ?"(*Ser.* 392, 3). From these proofs the fact emerges that confessions before the priest—indeed, also the avowal of one's innermost sins—and consequently private confession, were already held to be divinely instituted and necessary in the first centuries after Christ, and that private confession, alongside public confession, therefore existed already at that time.

However, throughout the Middle Ages, from the time of the Fathers until the Fourth Lateran Council, auricular confession is attested to by so many historical documents that the assertion that *that* Council first introduced it can only be explained by crude ignorance or effrontery. One reads of special father-confessors to princely figures, of clerics in the army who had to hear the confessions of the soldiers, of bishops who on account of the mass of penitents coming to them referred their confessions, as an exception, to members of the Regular Clergy. Then come admonishments and ordinances concerning confession in penitential texts and at councils, as well as teachings of theologians regarding it. Just as these prove the use of confession in the Church and the conviction of its divine institution and necessity, so do they form in their totality a *titulus praescriptionis* regarding the matter. In short, confession existed from the beginning, and there is no "moment" in the history of the Church when it first appeared. (Wetzer and Welte's *Kirchenlexikon*, Second Edition, Vol. 2, 227ff, Freiburg, Herder, 1883).

There is no truth to the idea of there being a "non-evangelical moral constraint" with confession, and also just as little to its being an "invention of priests." If it truly were so, who could be supposed to have been in a position to impose such an "invention" upon the entire Christian world, West and East, since the Christians living under the Oriental Schism also still have Catholic confession? I ask you, assuming the case that at a given time in our Christian past Catholic confession did not exist, and that suddenly it came to someone's mind to demand of people that "from now on, you have to make known your sins to the priest, even the most secret ones," would people, quite naturally, immediately have welcomed this thoroughly "pleasant" novelty, and would it have been introduced into the whole Church without further ado? Or, perhaps, at the end of the day, this actually might not have happened?

To cap things off, would there not have had to have been an expression of astonishment, a questioning regarding why and where such a demand had been written, and the reason for it not having existed beforehand; a murmuring, a storm of indignation, strife, discord, divisions? In any case, the introduction of such a novelty would not have proceeded so peacefully that no trace of it whatsoever should have remained in the chronicle of history regarding the who, the where and the when of the matter. Hence, the question regarding who "invented" confession, and when and where was it "invented," is what the *inventor* of this "invention of priests" would have to answer and to prove.

And then, once again, it is said that *priests* invented confession! It is of course a great comfort to the priest to sit for long hours in the confessional, listening attentively and patiently to dozens, often a hundred or more penitents, one after the other, giving counsel, consolation, warnings and so on, to each according to his need, and this for week after week, year after year, by winter frost and summer heat! It certainly must belong to the special comforts of the priest to travel many miles away, not infrequently during the night, by storm and bad weather, in order to hear the confession of the sick and dying. Still more appealing is this occupation in military hospitals, on battlefields and in houses troubled by Plague, by Yellow Fever, and by cholera epidemics, among lepers and the like. Indeed, if confession had not already been "invented," without a doubt priests would still now "invent" it in order to gain access to all such delightful comforts.

How can someone in the Protestant camp really be so thoughtless as to believe the most hair-raising nonsense where doctrines or institutions of the Catholic Church are concerned!

But, honestly, what about the impossibility of counting up all of one's sins? This objection, also found in the Augsburg Confession (1, 11), is just as inane as all the others. It rests on a complete lack of knowledge of what the Church demands from the penitent. The Protestant theologian, Karl Hafe, a zealous combatant against Rome himself, admits as much. He confirms that the Catholic rule only demands the avowal of those truly serious sins that one clearly and definitely recognizes after a rational and thoroughgoing investigation of his conscience. He describes Catholic confession essentially correctly in this manner:

> The first condition for forgiveness of sins is contrition; that is to say sorrow for the sins that were committed...The second act is confession according to the divine institution. This entails, on the one hand, as being necessary to salvation, the avowal before the qualified priest of all those mortal sins not already confessed (with any circumstances essentially affecting the moral guilt), and then of all venial sins, as far as the sinner, after careful self-examination, is conscious of them, as being something salutary. On the other hand, there is the judicial verdict given by the priest according to his power of jurisdiction, under unconditional maintenance of the secret of confession.

And so it is. God does not demand anything impossible of His children, and His Church just as little. It is not necessary to confess venial sins—that is to say, small faults, weaknesses and imperfections—which, although they do indeed offend God, still do not kill the soul. The devout reception of Holy Communion or an act of genuine repentance or of love for God is, thanks to the merits of Christ, sufficient to purify the soul of these less significant stains. Nevertheless, every good Catholic, in accord with the advice of the Church, takes care to confess these as well, insofar as he remembers them through the examination of his conscience.

Even if confession is an act of humiliation of human pride that always runs against one's natural inclinations, it is not as hard as even those who have only learned of it theoretically commonly assume. Moreover, there is no requirement of mentioning each sin of the same kind; these may be summarized. Thus, for example, the penitent may say: "I confess gross disobedience of my father or my mother," or: "I pretty much allowed myself to get seriously angry," and so on, for so often. For it is at this juncture that the penitent indicates the number of times that he fell according to his best knowledge; and so he confesses all the remaining mortal sins that he knows he is guilty of committing.

Father von Hammerstein recounts (*Errinerungen*, p. 104) the day of his conversion:

> After the conclusion of the ceremony [the act of profession of the Catholic Faith], I withdrew into my quiet little room and it seemed to me that I could finally, for once, freely breathe a sigh of relief, as though I now really had the ground under my feet; as though a hundred-pound heavy burden had been taken from my heart. With abundant joy I fell on the neck of Graf G. who entered soon afterwards to greet me.
>
> Still, there was one difficulty that I had yet to overcome: my first confession, which had to embrace my whole previous life. I was so fearful of this that I was close to passing out. I did not know how to proceed, and I had absolutely fantastic ideas of the penance that was generally prescribed. At the very least, I thought I would have to kneel several hours on peas or carry out similar acts of penance. I therefore knelt down but did not know how I should begin. At that time, the general formula commonly used to begin the act of confession was unknown to me.
>
> However, Dr. Heinrich, to whom I confessed, soon helped me, said the formula for me, questioned me regarding this and that, and, giving me as a penance at the end a small prayer to recite, absolved me in the place of God from my sins. And, with that, the entire terrible operation was finished. I had not imaged that, in practice, it would be so easy!

I can add that exactly the same thing happened to me at the general confession that followed my conversion.

The venerable Jesuit Father Wenniger, who died several years ago—a German-American missionary whose *Meditations* are held in honor not only by Catholics but also by many Protestants—reports in his *Experiences in America*:

> A Frenchman lay ill in bed. Although in his sixties, he had still not gone to confession, since he thought that it was of no use to him, being in no way in a condition to stir up an act of contrition. I came to see him and began to hear his confession. Experience had already often shown me that people who have not confessed have a conception of confession that makes this seem impossible to them. Therefore, it is best that the priest immediately sounds them out when he has them alone in his presence. Usually they have already felt the need for confession in their hearts for years, and by questioning them, the pus that squeezes out of the ulcers of their sins does so only to their very great relief.

> This approach means that they sometimes give their initial answers as part of a simple dialogue at a table in a room as well as in a confessional. They then are completely surprised when suddenly they are told: 'Well, will you look at that; now you have confessed. Kneel down and I will give you absolution!' When they then kneel down, you always have more opportunity to ask diverse and more delicate questions to complete the confession and awaken contrition.

> When I finished speaking with this old Frenchman as he lay there in his bed, I took a depiction of the Crucifixion into my hand and reminded him of what Christ had endured for him until He finally today could embrace him now as a redeemed soul. Then, all of a sudden, the sick man looked up at me and at the Cross and cried out: 'My God, my God, what is this that I feel? It is contrition. Holy God, a miracle! For the first time in my life I feel contrition!' Then, after sixty-eight years, the first tears of contrition fell

from his cheeks. Indeed it is really then, if ever, under such circumstances, that the priest confidently utters the words: 'I absolve you of your sins.' Soon afterwards, he died.

But is it possible that the priest can make use of what he has learned in the confessional to the disadvantage of the penitent? The priest is bound to absolute secrecy, not only for conscience's sake, due to the command of God, but also through the law of the Church, which threatens him with the most harsh punishment, with immediate dismissal, with the most rigorous acts of penitence. And when exactly has a Catholic confessor violated the seal of confession? Let someone bring up a single case in which this can be proven. On the contrary, there are not a few cases that can be proven where a confessor preferred martyrdom and death rather than to betray one word of what he heard in the confessional.

Therefore, the loving God, according to Catholic doctrine, cannot pardon a sinner without the mediation of a Catholic priest! This rather bizarre contention has also already been expressed on the part of Protestants. A splendid "Catholic doctrine" indeed! But the Council of Trent says something different. If the Catholic Christian in need of confession finds no confessor who can, as he is duty bound to do, absolve him, then an act of *perfect contrition* can suffice for his reconciliation with God. The Council says (14, 4), "Contrition through love, is sometimes perfect, and then it reconciles a man with God before he actually receives this Sacrament [that of Penance]," on the sole condition that the penitent has a genuine determination to go to confession when it will again be possible. However, if it is not possible, then he is justified even without it.

The great English convert, Cardinal Newman, writes:

How many souls there are that feel depressed, anxious and abandoned and whose only need is to find a being to whom they might be able to disclose their innermost concerns, unheard by the rest of the world! These want to come out, but the souls in question cannot bring themselves to express them to those with whom they must regularly deal each day. At one moment they would like to speak, and at another they again would not. They would like to utter their concerns, but yet in a way that no one might know it. They would like to speak to someone who would take it upon himself to hear them without afterwards being contemptuous of them; someone who would simultaneously bring them advice and sympathy. They would like to rid themselves of a burden, be consoled, have the certainty that there is someone…to whom they might come, when necessary, from time to time, escaping from the world in order to open themselves regarding their concerns again.

How many Protestants would be cheered by such a boon, totally apart from all considerations regarding a sacramental rule or an absolution or an offer of grace! If there is in the Catholic Church an idea coming straight from Heaven, truly, next to that of the Most Blessed Sacrament of the Altar, and considered even from the standpoint of a mere idea, it is penance! *And it is actually there…* Oh, what a soothing peace embraces us there [in the confessional]; a peace that the world can neither give nor take away! What a sweet peace, refreshing to the heart, spreads over the soul, eliciting tears of joy—the oil of bliss, as Scripture calls it—when the penitent finally stands up, reconciled with God, freed forever of his burden of sin! (Newman, *The Present Position of Catholics*, p. 351)

How true that is! Penance accommodates one of the deepest needs of the human heart. The Lutheran Pastor Evers, already cited earlier, admits: "The wish to be able to confess and to be certain that the absolution spoken by someone undoubtedly given full powers to do so would actually be granted to me was one of the most powerful of the motives leading me to the Catholic Church." And he adds to this:

Should the good friend who prophesied to me that

after twenty to forty auricular confessions I would have had enough of Catholicism catch sight of these lines I am now writing, let him, through them, receive my warmest greeting and the assurance that the institution of confession practiced by the Catholic Church has proven itself to me to be such a boon and so strengthening of a medicine that I make use of it weekly. I draw forth both from it as well as from Holy Communion a continually new strength for overcoming not just temptations that come to me from the external difficulties of my status, but also for the eradication of the deepest-seated roots of the weeds of the Old Adam. (*Katholisch oder Protestantisch*, p. 31)

In another passage where he speaks of Lutheran spiritual direction (p. 27), he says: "The experiences that I had in previous congregations and that I heard from the mouths of other clerics regarding this matter convinced me that so-called spiritual direction without the confessional as a basis is more or less that which medical care would be if the physician never asked nor examined the patient nor was allowed to prescribe a diet for him." Furthermore, he describes the education of children and the moral mischief and vices that he found to have made wide inroads among youth, and how he came to believe that the Lutheran cleric stood completely helpless and powerless in the face of spiritual direction *without* the confessional.

Pestalozzi says:

I just recently asked my good neighbor L. von H. why so few examples of abortion occurred among the people of Freiamt [in Switzerland]. 'Confession is responsible,' was the answer. 'No, we are not permitted to do this, as you are. I was also young once, but they [the priests] talk to you so very much alone and with such heartfelt feeling. They repeat to you so often and so solemnly and with advice that is not meant for the moment alone, but simply and properly of what remains to be done by you and what has been left hanging in the balance that it helps if such a disaster should take place. The priest in confession always easily gets to the bottom of an issue beforehand; he watches for the beginnings of a problem where someone is shying away from it or ashamed of it. And then there is also this fact: they do not stop instruction by us when children are fourteen or fifteen years old. Jesus, Mary! They say that spiritual direction should actually only then properly begin for them.'

There is a truth in this answer, and if confession may indeed have been misused, nevertheless it has in its nature certainly great strengths for the education of the people. The Reformation broke the tie that linked the people to the ear of the spiritual director. Daily, more and more, due to the consequences of the generally and unconditionally discarded use of confession, a close knowledge of the parishioners was lost, and the intimate relationship that truly bound together the hearts of priests and people was equally and visibly enfeebled … In our hearts, the pastors of our land have in many ways been reduced to the level of learned preachers incomprehensible to the people; they have been handed over to the mockery of everyone, even when in his most miserable and most base mood; even to the mockery of the most unworthy functionary in the countryside, as well as to that of every rich man. (*Sämtliche Werke*, VIII, p. 5)

Oh, how *rational* confession really is, even when looked upon simply as a means of instruction! How much it eases the educational task of conscientious parents! I can speak here out of my experience as the head of a large family. Supervise your children as much as you can, inculcate in them the law and the fear of God from their most tender years onward, strive with all zeal to accustom them to know that they are always in God's presence: that God is standing by them in all their works, words and thoughts. Yes, certainly that is all necessary in order to protect them from sin. Yes, without that no confessional will help.

But will it be enough? In the silence, will an evil habit, a vice perhaps creep into them without your knowing it? "God is with you"—and yet God is "far away," and the child is not necessarily "with Him." And, after all, He "does not hear confession."But the priest "hears confession," visibly, palpably and audibly. Moreover, the day when the child must appear before his confessional bench is never very far away. In his school years, the child must expect every day to be called before it. Afterwards, prudent parents continue to urge him to go frequently to confession. Thus there is added to the fear of the "distant" God the fear and the shame of the "nearby" confessor in the moment of temptation. What will good Father X say when he hears that from you!

Far be it from me to claim that the confessional, even when accompanied by a good education of the children in the parents' home and in school, always deters them, and from all sins. But I do claim that it does, on a daily basis, prevent innumerable sins, and that it is especially due to the confessional that certain particular moral aberrations which widely pollute youth in the rest of the modern world are extremely seldom, if not totally unknown, among the young people in good Catholic regions.

With this, I believe that I have sufficiently demonstrated to you that confession is thoroughly "evangelical"; that it has been practiced and maintained from the beginning of Christianity; and that it is extremely rational in all of its demands, means, and goals.

May God protect you! Your H.

~Chapter 9~
Purgatory: Anti-Biblical Blasphemy

My Dear D.,

So this question becomes "ever more interesting" to you. Still, you fear that through your "ever new questions" you are taking up too much of my time. This concern is groundless. I will answer you joyfully for as long and as much as you might wish. Hopefully, things will not turn out for me in the end as they did with Blessed Alban Stolz, who, in his splendid *Erziehungskunst* (p. 21), speaking of the obstinacy of youth with respect to the prejudices that they had learned, recounts the following tale:

> When I studied in Heidelberg, a student of a Protestant denomination made a disparaging remark to me about something that he had noticed in Catholic worship. I pointed out to him the meaning and the utility of the manner in which it was conducted. Since he could not figure out how to make any further objection against it, he merely said: 'I will grant only this: that the Protestant Faith is by far more excellent than the Catholic.' His prejudice was so firmly implanted that he even expected this admission to be made by Catholics themselves.

What do I think of Purgatory? Now it goes without saying that the Catholic doctrine of Purgatory is as certain a truth to me as all the other doctrines of the Catholic Church. And the same also holds true for the history of this doctrine as with others: that it has continuously been present in the Church of Jesus Christ, is completely in accord with Scripture, and that it is extremely rational as well. However, before substantiating my conviction to you, I will first sum up what we Catholics actually believe about Purgatory.

Purgatory—the place of purification—is a location where the souls of each of those departed believers who have died either in a condition of venial sin or have not yet given to divine justice a complete satisfaction for mortal sins, are cleansed through their suffering for gaining Heaven. In short: it is a temporary abode for those souls who are too good for Hell, but not yet good enough for Heaven.

You transcribed for me a passage from Luther's *Tischreden* (*Table Talk*, Reclamsche Ausg., 229, 230), in which he says that Purgatory diminishes and eclipses the merits of Jesus Christ, and that it is "conceived out of nowhere" (and, hence, not in the Bible). "Ambrose, Augustine, Jerome, did not believe in Purgatory." This passage does, in fact, contain the Protestant objections against Purgatory *in nuce* [in a nutshell]. What is in question is only if they are correct. Let us see if they are.

According to Catholic doctrine, the sorrows of the poor souls in this place of cleansing have no power in and of themselves: just as little intrinsic power as do the penitential works of the living. They receive their cleansing power first and foremost from the work of Redemption of Jesus Christ. The objection that Purgatory detracts from the merits of our Savior stands, accordingly, on weak footing. It is rendered completely moot through the fact that the doctrine of Purgatory is founded upon the Bible, God's Word itself, and that the Church from the beginning—and thus in the days which according to the Protestant vision "she had not yet been tainted by human additions"—possessed this teaching.

Now Luther maintains the opposite in the passage that you offered to me. But that same Luther wrote the following in other places: "One must firmly believe in Purgatory, and I know that it is very true that the poor souls suffer unspeakable pains there and that we must come to their aid through prayers, fasts, alms and all of the other means in our possession." (Ed. Lat. Wittenberg, P. 7, p. 7). Elsewhere he says:

> I am convinced that there is a Purgatory. All of the blabbering of heretics on this subject makes no impression on me. I know that in the fourth century St. Augustine in the ninth book of his *Confessions* wrote that he prays for

his father and his mother and that he desires prayers from others for them. He teaches me that his mother in her last moments asked him to remember her at the altar. He tells me, more or less, that the same sentiments were those of St. Ambrose. But even if there had been no talk of Purgatory at the time of the Apostles, would we have to conclude from this that the faith of so many centuries was false, as the heretic Pikard, who came into the world a mere fifty years ago, has done? (*Dissert. de Indulg.*, Ibid., P. 1, p. 112)

Luther is correct in these latter remarks; not in those of his *Table Talk*. St. Augustine, whom he cites—once in favor of and at another time against Purgatory—writes, among other comments, clearly and explicitly: "Those who have not tilled their field well and have allowed thorns to proliferate, will, after this life, experience either purification through fire or eternal death." A long series of other Fathers from the first centuries testify to the same doctrine, including Tertullian, Cyprian, Origen, Eusebius of Caesarea, Arnobius, Basil, Ephram of Edessa, Cyril of Jerusalem, Gregory of Nyssa, Epiphanius, John Chrysostom, and also Ambrose and Jerome.

Just as eloquent as the writings of the Fathers are an abundance of inscriptions in the catacombs that testify for the contested doctrine. The oldest liturgies already invariably contain prayers and *mementos* for the poor souls. Furthermore, in the oldest *Sacramentarium* (around 450) there are to be found six different Mass formularies for the deceased, a sign that the offering of the Holy Sacrifice of the Mass for their purposes must at that time already have long existed. Tradition is completely united on this point. Reports of it are so copious and so evident that many "Reformation" teachers such as Calvin, Peter Martyr, Daltier, Forbes and Bingham have acknowledged it.

And yet Purgatory is said not to be Scriptural. Let us take the Bible itself into our hands. We read there in the Second Book of Maccabees 12:43-46: "After a collection had been made, Judas sent 12,000 silver drachmas to Jerusalem so that a sacrifice might be offered for the sins of those who had died, since he thought this good and pious for the Resurrection. For if he had not hoped that those who had fallen would rise again it would seem superfluous and useless to pray for the dead... *It is therefore a holy and salubrious thought to pray for the dead so that they may be freed from their sins.*" With these words the belief in an intermediary state between bodily death and the "Resurrection," the entry of the soul into Heaven, is clearly and explicitly expressed.

In order to evade the impressive conclusiveness of these written passages, you will probably object that the authenticity of the Books of Maccabees is doubtful. But the early Church considered them canonical; Clement of Alexandria, Cyprian, Isidore, Augustine and other Fathers produce the most certain evidence in their favor. Still, supposing that the entire early Church had made a mistake in this matter, and that you (?) know better, nevertheless you have to allow for the fact that the Jews of the time clearly believed in a place of purification. There is not a word found in the Bible indicating that Christ and the Apostles rejected that belief. And the Fathers saw still further indications of the doctrine of Purgatory in the Old Testament in Tobias 4:18, Ecclesiastes 7:37, and Psalms 65:12.

Meanwhile, let us turn to the New Testament. Paul says: "Every man's work shall be manifest; for the day of the Lord shall declare it, because it shall be revealed in fire; and the fire shall try every man's work, of what sort it is.If any man's work abide, which he hath built thereupon [on the foundation of Christ], he shall receive a reward.If any man's work burn [wood, straw, stubble], he shall suffer loss; but he himself shall be saved, yet so as by fire (1 Cor. 3:13-15).

The early Fathers, Origen in the third century, Ambrose and Jerome in the fourth, and Augustine in the fifth, referred to this passage. "Wood, straw, stubble," the work that "burns" is the imperfect building material—the discussion here is of builders. They are the venial sins from which the soul must be purged "as through fire." In Matthew 5:25 and, respectively, in Luke 12:58-59, we also read of the warning of the Lord that so long as we are on the path to the Judge, we are able to correct the injustice that we have committed against our neighbors; but that whoever fails to do so will "be thrown into prison and will not be released until he has paid the last farthing." If some may say that the prison that is under discussion here is Hell, then one must respond that the pains of Hell last eternally, and in Hell, therefore, clearly "the last farthing" can never be paid.

In Matthew 12:32 the Lord speaks of the sin against the Holy Ghost, which "neither in the present nor in the future life will be forgiven." You must concede, with Augustine (*De. Civ. Dei*, XII, 24), that this remark would be superfluous if there were no sins at all which even after death—in the future life—could be forgiven. Then again, Holy Scripture says in diverse passages that God will give to each and every one what he earns; but that nothing unclean can enter Heaven. Is it indeed conceivable that God would eternally punish a man who was stained at the time of his death with a small sin—for example, "an idle word"— just as he would someone who had died in the committing of perhaps a murder or an act of adultery?

There are diverse passages in the Bible that solidly justify the belief in Purgatory. The early Church also already understood these passages as doing so. On the other hand, Holy Scripture contains nothing that testifies against this belief. The phrases that are cited against Purgatory on the part of Protestants prove nothing contrary to it. They point to the words: "Blessed are the dead who died in the Lord. Henceforth, the Spirit says, they will rest from their labor, for their works follow them." These blessed ones, who are lauded as "the dead who die in the Lord," are precisely those completely stainless souls, free of every sin, who departed from this life in a state of perfect grace. They also hold up against us Ecclesiastes 11:3: "When the tree falls towards the south or the north, wherever it falls, there it remains lying." This passage simply illustrates the fact that death holds sway over the final, eternal destiny of man. He who dies in mortal sin is certain of Hell; he who dies in a state of grace is certain that his last destination is Heaven. Obviously, the existence of

Purgatory is in no way thereby put into question. You may say that you understand these passages otherwise. The problem is that what is involved here are not conceptions, but, rather, proofs. You would have to prove that this passage of the Bible, or others, testifies against Purgatory. Can you do that?

Apart from this, the idea of a place of purification is far older than Christianity. We find it already among the pagans, as, for example, among the ancient Persians, the Greeks and the Romans. Virgil describes for us the place of residence where the dead do penance for their faults (*Aeneid*, VI) until: "The tear-stained multitude, their exile at an end, embraces, after many years, the long-desired shore."

I have already touched upon the fact that the Jews of the Old Covenant also believed in Purgatory. Drach says (*De l'harmonie de l'église et de la Synagogue*, I, p. 16), "Since the earliest days, the Synagogue prayed for the dead." The Moslems do the same. All of the liturgies of the ancient oriental sects—the Nestorians, the Jacobites and the Copts—contain prayers for the departed. Yes, even the majority of the Protestants, despite Luther, Calvin and other Reformers, accept the existence of a place of atonement.

Even the Lutherans would have to admit that there is an intermediary condition between life and eternal bliss if they would only draw the consequences from their own confessional writings. Does the Augsburg Confession not teach that the souls of the just do not reach Heaven before the resurrection of the dead? So where do these souls go in the meantime? They are certainly not in their graves, and just as certainly not in Hell. Where are they? What are they doing? Some Anabaptists say that they are sleeping. But Calvin protested. According to him, they are awake.

> Nampon appropriately asks, "Is it then possible that they seek with all the fire of their desire the sight and the possession of God; they, who on the earth, said with the Apostle (Philipp. 1:23): 'I have a desire to be dissolved to be with Christ?' Is this daily cheated desire not a true Purgatory of similar duration for each and every soul, and

just as long as the duration of the world for all of them?

Those who have them sleeping, or who, like Reinhard in his *Dogmatik*, suppose that they are numbed and unconscious due to death, maintain that on the Day of Judgment they, in but a moment, will be purified of all of their stains and put in a condition to enter Heaven. Here we also find a Purgatory, even if it does not possess the name. Furthermore, it means giving to God the duty to do what He does in a moment, as He does with everything else, in weight, number and measure. Others, such as Schlosser, Herder, G. Monod, and so on, revert to metempsychosis (transmigration of souls). The Oxford School accepts an intermediate condition between Heaven and Hell where souls are purified from their stains by torments that they themselves bring about. Jung Stilling calls this Hades. According to the eye and ear witness of Swedenborg, Purgatory is the 'third condition, through which the souls of the deceased wander, and in which they are prepared for entry into Heaven....' Finally, a great number of rationalists, among whom one can cite Ammon, Klaiber, Hencke, Wegscheider, Chenevière, Coquerelle, etc. want only a temporary Hell for punishment of the evil; that is to say only a Purgatory. (Nampon, *Kathol. Lehre*, Regensburg, Mainz, II, 262-264).

Thus the human spirit gropes uncertainly, here and there in the semi-darkness and on the unsteady foundation of misbelief, to find once again a lost truth that was in the possession of so many people through long ages, and for whose possession, after all is said and done, it still feels an unclear need.

And, in fact, this truth is a need, a postulate of reason; at least of true reason, reason of the kind that places both God's holiness and justice as well as His wisdom and mercy before the eyes. Is it not a daily occurrence that men who have not been lacking either in faith or in virtue, but who have not yet been purified at the moment of death from all of their small sins and weaknesses though contrition and penance, are suddenly overtaken by their unexpected end? Such souls obviously cannot lapse into Hell, but they can also certainly not enter directly into Heaven. Thus it is unthinkable, because irreconcilable with the qualities of God cited above, that He should not have ordained an intermediate condition in which they will be refined to that stainless purity which enables them to enter Heaven.

And how consoling, how uplifting, how fruitful this belief is with respect to all that is beautiful and good! Not only the impartial reason left to its own devices demands this, but the heart as well. With what pleasure the human heart that bleeds at a gravesite would wish to do something more for the beloved dead! But how can it, if all human influence over the fate of the departed souls stops with death in every case? The silent sleeper, lying down below, was, in general, a good and pious man, but are you certain that his soul has passed over to the other side so purely as to be worthy of Heaven without any further cleansing? Or perhaps he was a great sinner, and yet, he was your father, your brother, and love compels you to ask the anxious question: did all go well between God and him in the last hour; will his soul be saved from eternal ruin? You often offended him, and you often saddened him. Perhaps you were an accomplice in many of his sins? Perhaps you could have held him back from some of them and you avoided doing so?

> Oh, love so long as you can love,
> Oh, love so long as you would like to love!
> The hour comes; the hour comes,
> When you stand at the gravesite and lament.

Oh, if you had only loved him more, this now so dearly lamented deceased one! If you could only have him back once more, in order to apologize for that unfriendly word, to make good all neglected proofs of your love. How you would want to give them to him from your hands now! But:

> The wind that blows now through the grass,
> It whispers softly: it is too late!

Too late! He has been taken away from your love forever.

Your teardrops fall fruitlessly; fruitless is your lament, your contrition is fruitless, at least for him, for his destiny has been fulfilled. The only consolation that remains to you is hope; a hope troubled by a tormenting uncertainty.

How completely different, how inexpressibly more consoling and more fruitful the mourning of the Catholic Christian! The faith in a place of purification transforms his tears into prayer, while charitable works, sacrifices and alms make his sorrow of assistance to the beloved deceased and therefore less bitter for him as well. A new exchange of life develops between our departed beloved ones and we who stand above the burial mound; a continuous exchange of proofs of love until our reunion in eternal bliss. Chateaubriand exclaims:

> A wondrous traffic between the living son and the deceased father, between mother and daughter, between husband and wife, between life and death! While I share my abundance with the poor, God, for my reward, frees my father, my mother, from the place of torments. The same alms that hand momentary bread to the unfortunate set a place on the table of the Lord for a soul, freed for eternity. (*Genie du Christ., Purgatoire*)

A Catholic cemetery lies not far away from my home. I take my favorite walks to visit it. Among the thousands who lie there, awaiting the day of the Resurrection, there are many whom I knew, this one or that one who was closer to me in my life than the others. I am drawn to them, not only by memory and the desire to mourn them, not only by my love for quiet seclusion and consideration of the perishability of all things earthly, but also by the firm awareness that I can still be of use to most of them, and because of this to myself as well.

And then, my memory, completely of its own accord, moves me from these tombs and builds a bridge to others, far away in my beloved German Fatherland. The mortal remains that these faraway tombs hold have indeed long decayed into dust, but the souls live, and with confident hope my loving intercessions are now also raised up to the throne of God for them, and I renew in myself the determination to rush to aid them the best way that I can in other ways as well.

Sometimes I take my children with me on my walks. And with what pleasure they pray there, even at the tombs of the dead whom they scarcely know by name! Indeed, these little ones approach still closer to things divine than we do. Many matters that we adults only grasp laboriously are understood by their innocent souls as givens. My little Leo—you know from earlier letters what a scamp he is!—once, early last year, was with me in that cemetery. Its numerous trees were back to life, and brightly feathered birds weaved in and out of them. The sweet, squirrel-like, field mice carried on with their funny games on the lawns and on the paths, and here and there the first flowers were in blossom. The things that were there for the frisky boy to look at, to astonish him, and to question! He would most of all have liked to chase after a gorgeous, golden little bird, in order, if possible, to catch it.

Yet look at this, how he, in total seriousness, devoutly kneels and prays at my side! Birds, trees and butterflies; none of them are there for him at this moment. And so he knelt there with me on many hills. When we left, I pointed along the path to a grave: "Here is where Mr. M. lies, a brother of Mr. F. whom you knew." He immediately said, "Oh, don't we want to pray for him as well?" There lay therein something almost like a quiet reproach, as though I had intended to pass by this grave. And yet, at the same time—praise be to God!—there is not a trace of sentimentalism in this boy. Still, he is a child, with an uncorrupted temperament. The belief in a place of purification and the love for the poor souls is, to such a child, so to speak, totally natural.

Love never ceases. It knows no "too late"—even at the side of coffins and graves—but only if instead of exhausting itself with useless sentimental sighing and crying, it undertakes noble works for the beloved deceased. For true love does not live through soft feelings. The sap of love is action.

With love—Your H.

~Chapter 10~
Faith? Yes. Reason? No!

Dear D.,

So now you candidly recognize that, at least to the degree that I have expounded the doctrines of the Catholic religion to you up to this point, there lies therein "infinitely more rationality" than you ever would have dreamed possible; that, "for the most part they also correspond to the teachings of the Bible, and that an insoluble contradiction between the two of them is nowhere to be discovered." Nevertheless, despite this fact, the truth of the Catholic religion "still by far" escapes you. You know that "human reason easily leads to errors in divine matters," and that whereas "the Scriptural proofs, insofar as they have up until now been presented, have cleared away many obstacles, behind every solved problem new ones continually arise." You see yourself "now more than ever before a sea of doubts and inquietude" and you might "almost have wished never to have touched upon this subject." But it has "all too powerfully gripped you to let the matter rest." You must and wish "now completely to get to the bottom of the business." The mere "quest for the truth," that, according to the phrase of Lessing, should be sufficient, no longer satisfies you. Rather, you admit, along with Goethe:

> If I knew the path of the Lord,
> I would truly follow it fully with joy!
> If one would lead me into the house of the Truth,
> I would never leave it again.

Still, who will "lead you into the house of Truth, along this apparently still endlessly lengthy path?" You do not want me to "feel the need for the patience and effort of perhaps still years-long services as a guide."

My beloved D! It was clear to me from the outset that our

correspondence on this subject—that, as you well know, I did not provoke, indeed that I did not enter into without serious misgivings—would have removed many of your prejudices against the Catholic Church from out of your path and shake your firmly Protestant standpoint. Your last letter has made it clear that that is already an accomplished fact.

As far as my "services as a guide" are concerned, they stand at your disposal as long as you want. But in the final analysis, in divine matters it is God alone who can lead one to a permanent destination. If the sun of God's grace does not illuminate you on the path upon which you have now entered, as near to the goal as you may come—and already you are now much closer to it than you believe—you will never recognize it. The best human guide and the clearest signpost that Tradition, Holy Scripture and conjecture can offer you can only lead you towards the goal, place it before your eyes; but it cannot bring it about that you see in that goal *the goal*. And even if you really do see and recognize it, that fact alone will never move your will to acknowledge, embrace and hold fast to the Truth that has been identified. You will never be able to do so without the grace of God. The battles and tribulations that await you would, without a doubt, confuse you regarding your perception and take away your courage and your strength.

A quest for the Truth! A love of the Truth! What exalted goods these are! A Lessing, a Goethe believed they possessed them. Did they really possess them? One who really did possess them, the noble Fr. Leopold von Stolberg, says somewhere:

> One does not love the Truth if he is not ready to sacrifice everything for it; if, whether the doctrines of the Faith or of morality are in question, one avoids illumination because this could disturb our inner peace, the enjoyment of one or the other aspect of our life, or wreak havoc with the relationships of our earthly existence. 'Sanctify them through Thy Truth' Jesus Christ prayed to the Father for His disciples before he entered into His death agony. Woe to us if we thwart His prayer! We thwart it if we prefer

anything to the Truth. This is the 'pearl of great price' that no one who is not ready to sell everything to gain it is worthy of obtaining.

And so it is. Our Lord Jesus Christ, the eternal Truth Himself, said: "Whoever loves father and mother more than me is not worthy of me." Whoever is not ready to sacrifice the most beloved object in the world for the Truth is not worthy of the Truth. If you wish to reach the goal, then you must implore light from above; and if you reach the goal, then implore that light for the courage and the strength to embrace it.

In one point you are still completely trapped by a Lutheran outlook, and that is in your assessment of reason. This perverse outlook also caused me not a few difficulties on my path to the Catholic Church. According to Luther, reason is "the bride of the devil." He says that: "in divine matters, that is to say in those that concern God, nature is stuck inside itself, is downright blind." It understands nothing other than "how to milk a cow, to build a house and to breed children." (*Tischreden*, Frankfurt, 108, 110ff.) "Reason so belongs to the devil that it causes great damage in matters involving God, and the greater and more skilled that it is, the greater the damage that it does."

This fear in the face of the use of reason "in divine matters" that is deeply rooted in the believing Lutheran, constitutes, next to the Lutheran teaching on the Antichrist, the chief bulwark against the perception of the Truth. Even if one has already come very close to the Truth, he backs away from it alarmed. He convinces himself that reason, this illusion of Hell, wants to play a trick on him. What a fatal confusion of the spirit! One must truly see the devil everywhere—that is certainly a genuinely Lutheran viewpoint—and here he is as well! But then he is also there in another way: in the modern, liberal development of Protestantism, in that rationalist reaction, that wants reason to be able to decide everything in divine matters.

The Catholic assessment of reason avoids both these extremes. "Whoever does not believe in divine matters anything other than what he can measure with his reason,"

Leibnitz says, "diminishes the ideas of God." (More correctly stated, he denies *true* reason). But the same profound thinker remarks: "Whoever wants to oust reason in order to concede the ground to Revelation alone would resemble someone who ripped out his eyes in order better to see the satellites of Jupiter with a telescope."

That is precisely the Catholic standpoint. The same God who said: "Without me you can do nothing"—and that also means being incapable of recognizing the Truth—also demands that our worship be a reasonable one (Romans 12:1). It is on these grounds that Chapter 4 of the Dogmatic Constitution of the Catholic Faith of Vatican Council [*Dei Filius*] asserts: "Not only can faith and reason never contradict one another, but they mutually help one another; for right reason proves the foundations of the Faith, and, illuminated through the light of Faith, it develops theological science. The Faith on the other hand liberates and protects reason from errors and equips this with diverse insights."

Writes "Gottlieb" in his *Letters from Hamburg* (Berlin, Germania-Verlag, 2. Ausl. 882ff), the reading of which I recommend to you:

> The Catholic Church expects no one in matters of religion to renounce the use of reason. The Faith that Christianity demands is indeed something to be accepted on the basis of its divine testimony; but it is at the same time also something requiring a rational acceptance. In order for it to be something rational, the perception of the presence of a divine testimony must precede it. And this perception must naturally support itself upon a personal insight. It must be a personal knowledge. Man must therefore make use of his reason in order to recognize that what lies before him is a manifestation of something from God, a special Revelation in history, a supernatural fact. Without question, a believing Christian should not accept a truth revealed by God on account of the fact that he understands it, and insofar as he understands it. He accepts

it on account of the fact that the all-truthful and all-good God has revealed it. He does this in humble submission of his understanding, for it is sufficient for him to know that God has spoken it. Through believing acceptance of Revelation, man finds the most beautiful opportunity to submit his reason and will to God the Lord. Besides, divine Revelation also contains within it a series of truths and duties resulting from the exalted supernatural purpose that God, out of His goodness, has most freely given to man, a purpose beyond all prospects that human nature, considered in and of itself, could have held out to him, and these only can be grasped through God's Revelation and in no way through human reflection. Here, once again, there lies a call for the submission of human understanding to divine truth. Nature is already full of mysteries for man, and the natural world around us appears all the more full of mysteries the more that science progresses...The Lord God gave man reason; He constantly demands 'a rational service' from us. Thus, if He wants us to accept Revelation, He must clothe this in attributes through which it can be recognized as being certainly divine and differentiated from a false Revelation. And He did just that. The Christian Revelation, as this is presented by the Catholic Church, possesses the peculiarity that it is recognized all the more clearly as true and divine by all noble men; or better said, by all those of good will, the more that it is made an object of rational thought.... Reason itself recognizes the conscientious duty to accept it as a divinely identifiable Revelation.

Therefore, my beloved D., do not hide the light of your reason in this matter under a bushel, but make use of it diligently. Assiduously research the question still further.

And there is one further counsel I would like to give you. You have a Catholic Church very close to you. If you could see your way to it, regularly to attend sermons there, at least for a time, that would contribute not a little to your enlightenment. You do not have to fear that you will have to listen to uncharitable invectives against Protestants. For sixteen years I have been in many a Catholic Church, heard very many diverse priests preach many hundreds of Catholic sermons, but I have never encountered vicious polemics against those of a different faith. Above all else, my dear fellow, pray for the grace that God allows you to recognize the Truth, and pray, with the firm intention of following what it is that you find when you find it.

United with you in this prayer is your true friend, H.

~Chapter 11~
Catholic Intolerance and the Spanish Inquisition

My dear D.,

It appears to you to be "almost unbelievable" that I should assure you as I did at the conclusion of my last letter that the Catholic pulpit can be "so tolerant." How does this match up with the fact that just recently, at the forty-first General Assembly of German Catholics at Cologne—as you learned from the *Kölnische Zeitung* and other newspapers—one of the speakers "openly recognized intolerance as being a totally Catholic principle?" Surely, I do not wish to deny that: "tolerance itself is a child of the Reformation, although individual Protestants have infringed this principle and may still do so." Nor do I wish to hide from "historical facts such as the horror of the Spanish Inquisition and the St. Bartholomew's Night Massacre?" So there we have it; namely, the tale told us by Alban Stolz regarding his Protestant fellow students, here, in its latest edition!

Now, first of all, a few words about these "historical facts." No, I will not "run away" from them; by no means. I confess to you that if only one tenth of that which we heard in school and from "historians" like Paul Linbau were true, that I would profoundly lament it. However, the fact is that all serious historians today admit that by far the greatest part of this material is not true. Only sensation-mad scribblers of bad novels and Rome-eating theologians here and there still make use of these treasured old bogeymen.

The harshness and cruelties that took place under the Spanish Inquisition have been quite outrageously exaggerated. They are based primarily on the testimony of Llorente, a man who nurtured the most bitter hatred against the Church. But even if they were all true, one would not have the slightest grounds to lay their burden upon the Catholic Church, for the Spanish

Inquisition was in no way an ecclesiastical institution, but a state one: something that Protestant historians like Guizot, R.U. Menzel, H. Leo and even L. Ranke have long since conceded. It practiced a kind of state-organized anti-Semitism, since it was especially directed against a Judaism exploiting people under a Christian mask. It worked as an act of self-defense, conducted in an iron age, by a hot-blooded southern people. If your current day, Viking-like Ahlwardt, along with other Protestant Jew-baiters had been born three hundred years earlier and had had control of the authority of the State, would they perhaps have been more lenient? Besides, the Roman See always exhorted the Spanish Inquisition to act with clemency, offered refuge to many of those it persecuted, and took rigorous measures against false accusations and witnesses. But the Church can prevent all injustices among her children as little as the best mother can do so among her own children.

Similarly, the Church could not have prevented the so-called St. Bartholomew's Night or Paris Bloody-Marriage Massacre. She could not have prevented the rudder of the ship of state in France being at that time in the hands of a woman whose attitude could not have been less of a Catholic one [Catherine de Medici]. She was an imperious intriguer, who, despite the objection of the Pope, did not cringe from sacrificing the soul of her own daughter through her marriage to the Huguenot, Henry of Navarre. If she could do this for "Reasons of State," there could be no wonder, at least from a Catholic standpoint, that she might be similarly moved to assassination. Aside from more humble authorities such as Hagenbach and Baur, even Ranke recognizes candidly that it was not Catherine's concern for the Catholic Faith, but her concern for her power, for her personal position, that was to blame for the atrocity of St. Bartholomew's Night (*Histor.-polit. Zeitschrift*, Berlin, Duncker and Humblot, II, p. 601).

Now I am sure that you will also bring up the "horrible *Te Deum*" sung in Rome upon the arrival of the news of that atrocity. I have no intention of "running away from" this historical fact either; the real question, however, being why Rome thanked God for the news, and *how* it came to pass that the *Te Deum* was sung there. The French Court had simply fooled the Pope, as had happened before and continues to happen to Popes from Peter to Leo XIII, with regard to many matters, and this, today, despite the existence of railroads and telegraphs and newspapers. Rome was told that Coligny had conspired against the young King and the whole Court; that the "execution of the conspirators" had been merely an act of self-defense. And the *Te Deum* was also sung in Rome because it was thought that through the destruction of that alleged conspiracy, the imminent danger to the survival of the Church in France that its victory would have entailed had been removed.

Still, even had it been otherwise, and the Pope had really known the truth, what would this *Te Deum* have proved against the Church? Absolutely nothing! Just as little as if everything that has been said by biased authors regarding the Inquisition were true, along with all the other terrifying fairy tales concerning Roman intolerance spread with such skill since the beginnings of Protestant polemical activity.

The fields in which the Catholic Church labors have always sprouted weeds next to the good seed, and in the long line of popes there can be found here and there less worthy figures, even bad ones, among the very many noble and downright holy men. Once again, as I have repeatedly explained to you with respect to our debate over Papal Infallibility, we Catholics do not believe that the pope enjoys the privilege of being sinless, and just as little do we believe that all those who call themselves Catholic are good men.

The Church—and she alone among all sublunary institutions—possesses the means to sanctify men, but men possess free will and Catholics make bad use of this all too often, along with everyone else. I may have further opportunity to go into this subject, if you should feel the need to get to know the "marks" of the Church, especially the mark of sanctity. I refer you to a work entitled *Historical Lies: A Rebuttal of Common*

Distortions in the Field of History, with Special Consideration of Church History, published in numerous editions by Schöningh in Paderborn to deal with the historical aspects of the "difficulties" that you have mentioned and many similar ones that you may still subsequently produce.

If people really want to hold the Catholic Church responsible for the sins of her individual children, they must prove that the Church has caused such sins due to her commands or to her doctrines. And they must continue to prove this forever. However, the opposite is easy to demonstrate. Even sins against tolerance run directly counter to the Church's commands and doctrines. Those Catholics who might commit them would behave towards her as would children who are disobedient to their mothers.

The doctrine of the Church regarding tolerance is summarized most succinctly in the phrase of St. Augustine: "*Interficite errores, diligite errones*; Destroy the error; but love those in error." Every thinking person should immediately understand dogmatic intolerance; the fact that the Church and those who see the Truth in her doctrines cannot simultaneously love error; the fact that they must wish and strive to eradicate it.But the motive for this wish and striving is not hatred. It is love; the purest, most sincere love. And the weapons in this war of destruction, for every true Catholic, are only spiritual ones, instruction and prayer, the same weapons which I am presently using with you, my most beloved D., and out of love for you. Pius IX says, "Love demands that we pray fervently for the conversion of those in error."

If you cite the *Kölnische Zeitung*—one of the most dogged and unprincipled Culture War newspapers!—as a witness for the accusation of Catholic intolerance, I really do not know whether to take you seriously. If you are not yet ready to learn about things Catholic from Catholic newspapers, you should at least not draw your information from such notoriously anticlerical fonts; from newspapers which, admittedly, are the sources looked to on questions of belief and religion by "the propertied and educated classes." For they, like Liberalism in general, hurl their poisoned arrows against Catholicism only because they know full well that with the fall of Catholicism the *whole* of Christianity—which is what they really hate—would entirely collapse.

It is self-evident from what took place on the "Catholic Day" [an annual intellectual and devotional gathering] in Cologne, that it entered into no one's mind to declare intolerance of another sort to be a Catholic principle. The phrases uttered by the chairman of the local committee, Councilor Custodis, which the *Kölnische Zeitung* used its skill to try to poison, were these: "We are bound by the intolerance due to loyalty to our belief. There is only one Truth; what is not Truth is error. The Catholic Church is in possession of the Truth. We Catholics do not believe in the guilt of those with whom we live together but who believe differently from us. Those divided from us do not recognize our Faith because they, as a consequence of prejudices of no fault of their own, do not really know it. Therefore, although we are intolerant in our loyalty to our belief, we Catholics, in adherence to our Catholic principles, are the most tolerant and amicable men on the earth in our personal relationships." You can see from this, that this is really nothing other than what I have already told you regarding the solely *dogmatic* intolerance of the Catholic Church.

After having heard the *Kölnische Zeitung* on these words, you should find it interesting to listen to what a better, but still non-Catholic, newspaper says regarding them. The *Deutsche Adelsblatt*, the organ of the German Nobles' Association, in considering what had happened on the "Catholic Day" writes with an obvious eye to what the *Kölnische Zeitung* and other newspapers like it had argued:

> Incredibly, some believed that these propositions constituted a harsh offense against other denominations. We think otherwise. We believe that a Catholic loyal to his Faith cannot in the slightest way speak otherwise than, *mutatis mutandis*, a Protestant who is loyal to his own.

Each of the two denominations must, of course, claim to believe that its Faith is the true Faith. If not, it would simply not believe it. We really do not see any middle way. Such a middle way would be a 'half-belief.' A Protestant can only reproach a Catholic, or a Catholic a Protestant, for holding the canons of his Church to be the sole true canons if this middle way were the one being followed. Moreover, firm belief does not exclude mutual respect and recognition. The one denomination must simply concede to the other the same right that it claims for itself. If 'intolerance' is involved, this can only be one of personal faith. It cannot be an intolerance of moral constraint, of mutual suppression, of coercion, or contempt.

I believe that every reasonable Christian will subscribe to this proposition; certainly every Catholic Christian. Incidentally, let it be noted that the same newspaper made a further comparison between the "Catholic Day" in Cologne and the "Day of the Evangelical Union" that took place almost at the same time in Bochum. This comparison turns out much to the advantage of the former. "Out of simple love for justice, one thing must be mentioned," the *Adelsblatt* writes: "while in Bochum war drums and battle fanfares were sounded in a clear and even quite upbeat tone, in Cologne, anything that in any way could have indicated a provocation to the other denomination was avoided." Certainly this witnesses to the "Catholic Day" as having been both honorable as well as innocent. And the same is true in all Catholic assemblies, as well as from all Catholic pulpits, as it was in Cologne. Hopefully, you will follow my advice and convince yourself of this by way of experience. "The proof is in the pudding!"

"Tolerance is a child of the Reformation." You say that I at least will not deny *this* to be true. Actually, that fiction has already been disposed of through my explanation so far. Still, we will look to this yet further.

In the interim, this naïve student from Freiburg is being
tolerated by, Your H.

~Chapter 12~
Tolerance: The Child of the Reformation

Dear D.,

So, let us get back to that old fairy tale: "Tolerance is a child of the Reformation." You need somewhat more history, my dear D., and a somewhat freer and farther-seeing look into the living present; which, if possible, speaks more loudly to us than the past!

History—that is to say not the history destined for Protestant or secular schools, and other prejudiced writings that are falsely called historical—but actual historical writings that are only concerned with the determination of historical facts, the uncolored truth, and teach us about this.

I myself will back away from the podium for the moment, and first give the floor to a few witnesses who were more deeply involved in historical research than I am and may also be less suspicious to you since they were not Catholics but Protestants.

Guizot says:

> There are two main consequences of the Reformation: "first of all, the multiplication of sects and the disintegration of the unity of the religious community resulting therefrom; secondly, tyranny and the spirit of persecution. One can easily say to the reformers, 'you are urging people to anarchy, and then when that anarchy arises you want to tame and suppress it, and indeed through the harshest and most violent means.' One can easily say to them, 'you persecute heretics, and do so by means of an illegitimate authority.'

> "The supporters of the Reformation were indeed put in an unpleasant position as a result of their actions. If one blames them for having multiplied sects, they then condemn the sects. If one rebukes their spirit of persecution, they then plead necessity as an excuse. They

had the right, they said, to suppress error, for they were in possession of the Truth; their Faith, their institutions alone were legitimate. And when the sects persecuted by them objected: 'but we are only doing what you yourselves have done; we are splitting off from you, as you split off from the Catholic Church.' Then they were even more at a loss for justifying themselves, and usually answered only through a still worse persecution. (*Histoire générale de la civilization en Europe*, Leç. XII)

The English historian Hallam indicates, "The actual mortal sin of the Reformed Churches is the addiction to persecution; an addiction so great that every honorable man's zeal for their cause cools to the degree that his studies of this subject expand" (*Constitutional History*, V, I, c. 2).

Lecky, his Protestant countryman, and also an enemy of Catholics, remarks:

What should we say of people who in the name of religious freedom plunged their land into a sea of blood; who trampled underfoot the first principle of love of one's Fatherland by calling foreigners to their assistance (as, for example, by calling the Swede, Gustav Adolf, to Germany), and who, when they finally reached their goal, immediately introduced a religious tyranny as absolute as the one that they had brought down (!)? This was the position that Protestantism adopted for more than one hundred years...Nothing could be more erroneous than the statement that their [persecution] was only a weapon of necessity in a moment of danger, or an outbreak of natural indignation, or the inconsiderate maintenance of an older tradition. The persecution under the original Protestants was due to an explicit and positive doctrine that was dealt with in learned treatises, bound together inseparably with a great part of their new theology, developed by the most educated and far-seeing theologians, and brought to use against the most harmless as well as the most dangerous sects. It was the doctrine of the most glorious days of Protestantism. Those who are justly looked upon as the greatest of Protestant leaders are those who taught it. It was most clearly spread among those classes that were most saturated by Protestantism's dogmatic teachings. (*Rationalism in Europe*, V, 2, 59-61)

I could cite for you identical-sounding voices of those knowledgeable in Protestant history in abundance, but I want to write you a letter, not a book. And this letter itself may already grow to great length on its own steam.

If we delve into the historical facts themselves, we find the same phenomenon everywhere: the Reformation established itself with the most exquisite intolerance, with violent oppression of Catholicism and wild persecution of its proponents.

Let us turn our sights to Germany. A contemporary of the first part of the Reformation, Johannes Hoffmeister, the Prior of the Augustinians in Colmar, identified the method of the Protestant princes and city magistrates against their Catholic subjects and fellow citizens as follows:

Do the examples of Electoral Saxony, of Hesse, and other principalities of Germany, do the examples of so many imperial cities and that of Switzerland not sufficiently make clear what lies in offing for the Catholics when the heads of the sects, spiritual and secular, gain power to carry out publicly what their secret intention was from the beginning? They take from Catholics the possession of their churches, their cloisters, their endowments, their charitable institutions, their hospitals and their schools. They violently suppress Catholic worship, weigh down its exercise with harsh punishments, severely punish even those of their subjects who dare to participate in a Mass, or to have their children baptized Catholic, or themselves receive the sacraments even merely outside their territories... .Do not many of the sectarians engaged in overturning all public order declare that the Catholics should be exterminated with fire and sword because they are idol worshippers and blasphemers? (Janssen, *Geschichte des Deutschen Volkes*, III, p. 191)

Luther, who is so keenly held up by Protestants as a "liberator of conscience," warned the secular princes of his party and others of like mind against practicing tolerance towards their Catholic subjects. He insists, "In this matter, we cannot be concerned for the maintenance of temporal peace, for God would punish us for indicating to Him that we are displaying a readiness to aid the maintenance of such a great abuse. The Holy Ghost speaks quite seriously against such idolatry." (*Corp. Ref.* 2, 304ff).

What he calls upon the secular authority to do against the Catholic Church for the "pursuit of the Gospel" already emerges clearly from his writings On the Christian Nobility of the German Nation and *On the Papacy in Rome Against the Romanists in Leipzig*. Here he says:

I would be truly grateful if kings, princes and all nobles would close the roads to the traffic of that knave from Rome...It really moves one to pity to think that kings and princes are so lacking in devotion to Christ; that His honor so little moves them, that they allow such abominable disgraces to Christianity to get out of hand. At Rome they only become ever more nonsensical, constantly increasing each and every misery, so that there is no more hope on the earth except through the use of secular force to stop them. Since the Romanist [in Leipzig] again comes our way, I want to say more about this. (Altenb. U. I, 470-471)

Döllinger says that: "it was now reigning Protestant doctrine that the princes had supreme judicial authority over religion, teaching and the Church, and that each of them had the right and the duty to suppress dissident beliefs. On this, Lutherans and Reformed Christians were in agreement." (*Kirche und Kirchen*, p. 53). However Luther championed this doctrine not only against Catholics, but also against competitors in the

"Reformation" business. Hence, he admonished Duke Albrecht of Prussia in 1532 with respect to the Zwinglians: "Your Princely Grace should avoid such people and not tolerate them in your country, in accord with the advice of St. Paul and the Holy Ghost" (De Wette, 4, 349).

People in the other Protestant lands were robbed of their old worship in the same manner as well. In England, for example, (as Protestant authors such as B. Burnet report), the population could only be compelled to renounce the Catholic Church through the arms of foreign mercenaries. Martin Bucer assigned the secular authority the right to eradicate papal idolatry with fire and sword, and even to strangle women and children. (See, for example, citations in Janssen, *Geschichte des Deutschen Volkes*, III, 114, 191-192). Calvin called upon the Duke of Somerset as Regent of England to exterminate by the sword all those who opposed the new Protestant form of ecclesiastical organization. The Quaker, William Penn, estimated that in a short time close to five thousand people held for religious reasons were annihilated in English prisons.

Buckle, who is certainly reliable, says regarding Sweden: "Intolerance and desire for persecution reigned in no country like Sweden, which was doubly disgraceful because this came from a people that maintained that the foundation of its religion was the right to personally judge regarding its precepts."

An exceptional punishment was laid upon the celebration of the Holy Sacrifice of the Mass in all Protestant countries. In England, every Catholic priest who entered the country was subject to the penalties of High Treason. Its punishment consisted of the following: the delinquent was first of all hung, at once lowered again from the noose and cut open alive, disemboweled, and then finally quartered. The long list of martyrs—that actually only indicates executions taking place in Tyburn, in London—gives witness to how often this happened. Laity and even women were often executed in the most gruesome manner because they sheltered Catholic priests.

Protestant intolerance was also transplanted from Europe to

the New World. The history of the first century of British North America is simultaneously the history of a barbaric persecution of Catholics. Acadia (French Nova Scotia) had been inhabited for almost a century by a simple, pious, Catholic population of shepherds, when Louis XIV in 1713 in the Treaty of Utrecht ceded the land to England, and the Catholics living therein were at once driven from their homeland by murder and fire.

A no less tragic destiny was met by the Catholics of Maryland; the first British Colony in which full religious toleration had been introduced and practiced by the Catholics themselves. The Catholic Lord Baltimore, to whom King James I had handed over full, unconditional right of possession over the Colony, opened it voluntarily to "all who believe in Jesus Christ." His representative and councilors even had to swear to an oath never to impair freedom of conscience.Episcopalians, excluded by the Puritans from New England, found a home and a place in his legislative bodies in Maryland. The Puritans driven from Virginia sat on the same council with the Episcopalians and the Catholics.

The Protestant jurist Storey writes:

> It certainly says a lot on behalf of the generosity and the community spirit of this proprietor that he, in his fundamental political policy, included the teaching of general toleration and the equal legal rights of all Christian denominations, thus offering the first example of a lawgiver who invited his subjects to a free exercise of their religious convictions. This deed preceded the settlement of Rhode Island and earns thereby the enviable fame of being the first recognition of the glorious and imperishable right to freedom of conscience. (*Commentary on the Constitution*, Book I, Chapter 9, p. 106)

Religious freedom in countries with a population of mixed denominations is a social necessity according to Catholic teaching.

America's greatest historian, George Bancroft, also a

Protestant, writes:

Within six months, the Colony of Maryland had progressed further than Virginia in the same number of years...But far more remarkable still was the character of the governmental arrangements in Maryland. Every other country in the world had laws of persecution; the oath of the Governor of Maryland reads: 'I will in no way, neither myself nor through others, neither directly nor indirectly, molest anyone who confesses belief in Jesus Christ on account of religion....Protestants were also protected there against Protestant intolerance.... The history of Maryland is the history of benevolence and of tolerance. (*History of the United States*, ed. Routledge, p. 888)

And what was the thanks that was gained for all this? Already towards the end of the seventeenth century, Maryland Protestants provoked a revolt. They sought and managed to gain from King William, the Orangeman—who, in his "Decree of Grace," had granted freedom of conscience to "all Christians, with the exception of Papists"—the posting of a governor who then proclaimed the English High Church to be the state religion, pillaged the Catholics through taxation of the churches and preachers, declared them incapable of holding any position, and decimated them through persecutory laws, each of which was always more abominable than the others. A law was enacted in 1704 under the title: "Law for the Prevention of the Growth of Papism in this Province." In 1718 the "Law for the Further Prevention of the Growth of Papism," that had earlier been passed by the British Parliament under William II, took its place.

Here you have several provisions of that law, which was put into practice with fanatical rigor: Section One assigns a reward of one hundred pounds to anyone who "seizes and captures" a papist bishop, priest or Jesuit, brings him before the court, "handing him over for the saying of Mass or the exercise and performance of any aspect whatsoever of his office as a papist bishop or priest." Section 2 punishes with lifelong imprisonment "any papist bishop, priest or Jesuit who says

Mass or takes on the performance of any other act whatsoever that is appropriate to such a bishop, priest or Jesuit; or any other person confessing the Catholic Faith who runs a school or raises any children whomsoever, offering them instruction and board." Section 4 states that "every young papist man who does not within six months after he has reached his majority swear a certain prescribed oath [which is incompatible with the faith of the Catholic Church] will be declared incompetent to take over real estate through inheritance, his closest Protestant relative gaining it in his place; and that each and every person confessing the Catholic Faith should not be able to buy any land." Sect. 6 says that: "whoever sends children outside the country so that they can be raised in the Roman Faith should be punished with a fine of one hundred pounds."

Similar "tolerant" laws existed in the remaining colonies. I want to spare you the description of particulars from the bloody annals of that time. North American Protestants only took the first steps on the path to toleration for political motives, after something more than a hundred years, when the colonies during their War of Independence sought and received the help of Catholic France. But the cry of "no popery" by no means was stilled thereafter, and my older contemporaries can still quite well remember from the time of their youth wild "Catholic baiting" with murder and fire in this land of "full freedom and equality."

Still, let us call it quits with times and things of which we have no knowledge from our personal witness of them. Let us instead look around us in the living present and remember jointly-experienced incidents. Did you not yourself witness the glorious Prussian-German "Culture War," and the May Laws enacted by a Protestant regime and a popular majority, which robbed the Catholic Church in Prussia of its freedom to survive? A freedom, by the way, that had been guaranteed, for good measure, through the Prussian Constitution and the work of the King? In order to refresh your memory of the spirit of "tolerance" wafting through Germany at the time, I will cite here some "poetry" from those days. They sang this at the Canossa Festival on the Harzburg in the summer of 1876 with rowdy jubilation:

> "When the priests grew brazen,
> They headed towards the north of Germany.
> To the sound of trumpets leading them on,
> The Roman excursion made its way,
> Led by Herr von Ledochowski.
> On these crows pounced Minister Falk
>   [behind the May Laws],
> On the biggest rouge of all,
> Of the entire Center Party.
> This one had already long served
> As a volunteer in the clerical army,
> He had passed his Roman-Latin wind
> And blinded the Catholics.
> His name is Windthorst of Meppen."

That same spirit was cultivated at the time among young people. Hence, a popular "reader" that was also given as a prize to Catholic children at the Sedan Festival sported the following verses:

> "Doctor Falk the noble knight,
>   Wants to bring once more to the Emperor
>   What the Pope took off from him.
>   He drew up the May Laws
>   So that no longer the Chaplains
>   Might rummage and scamper through
>   the German land.
> Who has sung this song?
> Two masters of German youth,
> Those youth, who are joyful to live in this great era.
> Down with the Latin rogues!
> Cheers to the noble German hawk [Minister Falk]!
> Always hold your head up fresh and high in combat!"

This brutal quarrel, a true travesty of the much-vaunted Protestant sense of "tolerance," has indeed now lost its steam, at least insofar as the state authority takes part in it, thanks to the unanimous and stubborn resistance of the German Catholics. Nevertheless, the ignominious laws that were enacted still have not yet all been removed; the spirit from which they emerged still lives; it dominates your Press, it makes a ruckus in your "Evangelical Union"; it creates fuel for itself in the current battle against the Polish Catholics; it feeds propaganda for a German celebration of the three hundredth birthday of Gustav Adolf, the "evangelical" Swedish King and exterminator of Catholics, who, with his crude mercenary cohorts, brought so much want and misery to our Germany; and it manifests itself to the eye of the attentive spectator in innumerable other forms.

And how does it stand with us, here, in our land of the free and the equal? Here, also, this spirit of intolerance has by no means yet died out. Just now, it has again threateningly raised its head in innumerable secret societies of which the so-called "American Protection Association" is most mentioned. These bands, bound by terrible oaths, operate in the shadows to battle against Catholicism with every means at their disposal, seeking to exclude Catholics from all offices and legislative bodies, to destroy denominational schools, of which the Catholics have by far the largest number, and which they build and maintain while they are simultaneously taxed for the secular State schools; and yes, even to damage Catholics and where possible entirely to ruin them financially. They do this, although such policies run counter to the clear letter of the fundamental American law, without any impressive counter-movement on the part of Protestants making itself heard! And where there are reports of Protestants who are against these brutal, unconstitutional endeavors, one gets the impression that they generally are less due to tolerance as to political or national party considerations.

In short, in the past and in the present, both in the Old and the New World, there is little to detect of the infant named "tolerance" to whom "the Reformation" is supposed to have given birth, but rather, quite the opposite. The Church is still hated and persecuted by the world, and she is still hated and persecuted by Protestantism. And that, for me, was one of the first marks that I recognized of her origins in the silent, suffering, God-Man, Jesus Christ, when I undertook more serious historical studies and a more extended survey of present-day events.

The same is true for others. The English convert, Henry William Wilberforce, a friend of Newman, Manning and other leading voices of the Oxford Movement, says, in the farewell letter that he addressed after his conversion (1850) to his earlier congregation—he had been an Anglican Pastor in the Diocese of Canterbury—in which he cites the grounds for his change of Faith:

> I could bring forth many more arguments that the Catholic Church is the true one, but I will confine myself to one: the world hates the Church and has always hated her. I do not need to prove this, you know it and see it. You could be an Anglican or a dissenter; you could be affiliated with who knows which faction of a dissenting party; you could yourself found a new sect, without someone chastising you. Your friends, your relatives will perhaps laugh, shrug their shoulders, but that is really all. People may make fun of you, but no less esteem you, and certainly not hate you for such trifles. You do not even need to have any religion at all if that suits you, and your relatives and friends will say that that does not concern them.

> But if you become a Catholic, then you have to expect that the world will hate you. Your friends and your dearest relatives will abandon you, or, at the very least, they will treat you coldly. The gentlemen and ladies of high society will behave towards you as though they are permitted to treat you like anyone of no account on the street. In dealing with you they will breach the simplest rules of ordinary courtesy…

The manner in which one treats the Church as a religious society is still more extraordinary. The dissident sects can hold their meetings where they please. The residents where they do so know nothing of them or pay no attention to them. But the foundation of a Catholic Church disorients the country. Immediately controversy is stirred, unsettling sermons are delivered, all manner of calumnies and lies regarding the Faith and the worship of Catholics are spread about. Those who go to the Church are noted. If they are merchants, their clients leave them; if they are workers, they are driven from their jobs and their friends turn their backs on them at every moment. Everyone appears to be gripped by unease and terror. Catholic priests are the targets of the most cutting insults, the most outrageous defamations...

By the way, none of this is new to us, for when the Church of Jesus Christ was founded, the world was shaken. It hated the Church and feared her. It invented all sorts of strange and gruesome fables to use against her. It flared up at the sight of her like the demon when he saw that the Lord set to work to drive him out of the bodies of the possessed. When Christians entered a pagan city the inhabitants cried out: 'Those who incite riot have come here as well,' and, nevertheless, they could not resist a profound and mysterious appeal. Those whom God had chosen, one after the other, were drawn into the holy fold of the Church, and the world could not avenge itself on them except by accepting, spreading and believing unquestioningly all sorts of lies and defamations against the Christians, their priests, their religion and their heroes. It accused the Christians of hating the human race, of violating children, of drinking human blood in their churches, of gathering together in order to commit the most horrible crimes. It called their religion an odious, deplorable, abominable and infamous superstition.

Dear old Church! You are always the same. You have never changed. You are immovable because you are built on rock! And nonetheless the world hates and fears you! Do we not have the same scenario before our eyes? Have we not seen the same spectacle in the last three months? England has taken up arms. Meetings have been held everywhere. Lying and ridiculous expressions have been spread about, and the people who repeat them do so because they honestly believe them. But they should have gone back to their sources to confirm their authenticity before they blew their trumpets.

The cause of this movement was the naming of Catholic bishops for the most important English cities by the pope. I confess that these facts brought me a great consolation and firmly encouraged me. I see the world in a fury because the Lord has descended among men in His true Church. I see the shadow of the Cross in all this rage and in all this clamor, and where the Cross is, there Jesus is as well. I remember that He said: 'The servant is not greater than his Master. If they have persecuted me, they will also persecute you. If they have kept my word, they also keep yours.' The proof that the Catholic Church is the veritable Church of God is that all men hate her. She bears the mark of the Lord: 'Blessed are you when men revile and persecute you on my account, and lying, speak all manner of evil against you' (Matthew 5:11), and: 'The time will come that those who kill you think they are serving God' (John 16:2). To be good and to be called bad, to do good and to suffer evil, are the signs by means of which one recognizes the people of the crucified Jesus, and these signs are today as on other occasions, yes, more than ever, those of the Catholic Church.

I fear, my friend, that with this letter I have put your patience to a severe test. Yet I well remember how much pain it brought to my own heart when I had to admit that the ideas instilled in me with respect to the concept of tolerance were illusory. But it was precisely because I knew how hard it is for a Protestant to abandon this illusion, how deeply it is rooted in the traditional, Protestant consciousness, that I believed that I had to linger so long on this point.

Sincerely yours, H.

~Chapter 13~
Sola Scriptura (The Bible Alone)

My Dear D.,

The Mass, Indulgences, fasts, priestly celibacy and so on and so on! You don't find any of this in the Bible. Therefore, you say, either all this must be un-Christian or that Protestant principle according to which "the Bible alone" is the source, norm and rule of the Christian Faith, must be false. There is no third alternative. This is very true. And we hereby finally approach the cardinal point of the whole controversy. May I succeed, with the grace of God, to provide you full clarity in addressing it!

Should the Bible be the sole source, norm and guide to the Faith for individuals, it must doubtless be clearly understandable for everyone with reference to all that we must believe. But is this true? Let us put that question to the father of the German "Reformation" himself.

"If someone questions you," Luther says, "and says that Scripture is enigmatic, you should answer him that this is not true. There is no book that has been written on earth that is more clear than Holy Scripture." Yet towards the end of his life, he admitted: "No one should think that he has tasted Holy Scripture sufficiently if he has not himself ruled the Church for a hundred years together with the prophets Elias and Elijah, with John the Baptist, with Christ and the Apostles." He also writes: "We are students, incapable of fathoming a single verse from the Scripture, and it is only with effort that we succeed in understanding its very ABCs." And still further: "The Bible is indeed a pure, honest, malmsey wine; yes, a genuine, healthy medicine and refreshment. But when impure, evil worms come to it with their poisonous thoughts, infused in them from the devil, and then draw and drink from it, they spit out as malmsey what is actually vain poison, and that is why nothing but heresy and false teaching is taken and passed on from Scripture by them. For they claim to believe that all their erroneous stuff is grounded in Scripture, and affirm that it is taken from it."

I can furnish you with a set of further Protestant claims. Lessing, in his famous controversy with Pastor Götze, asks: "Can you deny, Herr Pastor, that only a few passages of the entire New Testament yield the same concepts to all men; that with some this concept, and, with others, another concept arises concerning the greater part of them? Which of these concepts are the correct ones? Who will decide? You say that the hermeneutic will decide! But which is the true hermeneutic? Are they all true? Or is none of them true? And this miserable, invalid approach should be the test of Truth?" (Lessing's *Werke*, VI, 97).

Hafe (in his *Polemik*, 2nd edition, 37) writes: "The mass of the population does not have the means of understanding, and therefore also cannot have the duty, and the authority to justify every believer independently drawing his proof of his Faith from Holy Scripture." Says Schenkel:

> If the earlier Protestant theology presumed the universal 'clarity' of Holy Scripture as an undoubted fact, it is because this presumption as yet did not have a notion of the indispensability of historical criticism. The diverse origins, worth and character of the individual writings must be explored. Only arrogance and lack of judgment could presume to be able to do so without further ado. It is only with the help of comprehensive linguistic and historical proficiency, thorough preliminary studies, and exercising the most intense and in-depth diligence that it is possible to ascertain the truth from compositions that belong to distant ages and have so often been misinterpreted through prejudices and party considerations. (*Christentum und Kirche*, Wiesbaden, 1867, I, 231)

Kant writes, "There is more logic in Roman Catholic Church life than among Protestants on this matter [of Bible reading]."

The Reformed preacher La Costa says to his fellow believers:

> Draw the Divine Word from the source (the Bible) itself, whence you can take it to yourself, pure and unadulterated. But you must, of course, not find anything in the Bible other than what we find in it.' Now, dear friend, tell us rather, what you find in the Bible so that we do not ourselves look unnecessarily, only to be told in the end, that what we thought we found in it was held by you to be an incorrect interpretation of it. (*Streit der Facultäten*, Rosenkranz, X, 316)

How indeed can the Bible be self-explanatory if it itself *confirms* such Protestant testimonies, the number of which can be augmented at will? And the Bible does in fact confirm them. Goethe remarks, "Peter already thought that there was much in the letters of St. Paul that was difficult to understand, and yet Peter was a completely different man than our current Lutheran superintendents." The passage in Peter that is in question (2 Peter 3:16) reads: "As also in all his epistles, speaking in them of these things in which are certain things hard to be understood, which the unlearned and unstable wrest, as they do also the other scriptures, to their own destruction." In the Gospel of St. Luke (24:45) we read: "Then he opened their understanding, that they might understand the Scriptures (the Old Testament)." When the Apostle Philip on his way from Jerusalem to Gaza asked the treasurer of Queen Candace, who was reading the Prophet Isaiah: "Thinkest thou that thou understandest what thou readest?" he answered: "And how can I, unless some man show me?" (Acts 8:30-31) And Philip, instructed and enlightened by the Holy Ghost, explained it to him. The court official believed his words and Philip baptized him.

The Bible therefore lacks clarity. It has need of interpretation. Saying, as one does, that "it interprets itself" is a thoughtless phrase. It is, as Schenkel indicates, "an improper figure of speech; the active principle in the process is human intellectuality." Rathusius, a representative of the more recent orthodoxy, writes:

The Bible has need of interpretation... Dr. Luther also would not have dared want to give the Bible to the people without interpretation. He gave the minimum of interpretation in his prefaces, in the chapter headings, and then quite splendidly in his references to parallel passages... Everywhere this makes the desire for still more interpretation notable. (*Halle'sches Volksbl.*, Aug., 1854)

But Schenkel, a spokesman for Liberal Protestantism, answers with inescapable logic:

Either the Scriptural teaching is in all of its essential parts so simple and clear that conscientious interpreters cannot conceive them diversely; that is the old Protestant teaching of the clarity and sufficiency of the text. If so, then the pressure for an interpreted text has no sense. Or, on the other hand, the text is neither clear nor adequate. Then Rome is correct, the Church authority must give the interpretation, and the Reformers who departed from the authority of the Church were wrong. Who gave them the right to set up their authority in place of that of the Catholic Church? (*Berliner Prot. Kirchenz.*, 17 February, 1855)

Resignedly, Perthes candidly responds to this alternative:

No prophet sent from God interprets the sublime mysteries [of Scripture]. No consistently reliable interpretation has come down to us from Tradition, we Protestants not holding the decisions of the earlier councils or of Catholic bishops as being greater than human statutes. And we would be illogical if we wanted to ascribe a higher credit to the Augsburg Confession. Luther arguably felt this to be the case, and all true servants of the Word feel the same. Because they cannot credit themselves with any gift of the Holy Ghost as direct illuminators of the text, they therefore call upon their congregations, in real distress: 'Inquire of the text yourselves; we also can only give you what we, through our inquiry, have received and acquired.' That is the sole standpoint of Protestantism upon which preachers who are honest men can rest. (Perthes, *Leben.* Gotha, III, 203)

Nevertheless, this "standpoint" does not in any way satisfy him. Just how much he must have felt its insufficiency emerges from the following. Perthes states:

A man all too easily forgets, or sells out, or alters the Word, or stares obtusely at it. Once again, he finds he has need of a helper in order to be able to grasp even that help that has already been offered. But who can lead him into the depth of understanding; who can resolve for him the sense of the words; who can preserve the Word and spread it? That is the great and difficult question. Scripture has need of protection against the arbitrariness of men, and man has need of an interpreter of Scripture. The institution that should resolve this two-fold need is the external Church. But where is she; who has her? …The laity, it is said, should allow themselves to be taught by the clergy. All well and good, but who teaches the clergy? …Does not every clergyman teach himself on his own, through the instruction presented him in scholarly form at the universities, in one way here, and there in another? Each of them starts again from scratch, and whether and what he makes of it depends on the good nature, poetic sense, philosophical sharpness, and devout heart of the individual. Were it not for shame and timidity in the face of the Catholic Church, how loudly, and how full of despair, would be the cries of believing Protestants for the help and authority of a Church whose voice we could hear ring out everywhere! (*U.a.D.*)

What was said above should alone be sufficient to substantiate for you that the Protestant principle of Faith is false. And yet we do not want to satisfy ourselves with this alone.

If the Bible alone were to be the source of the Faith, it must contain the teaching of Christ *fully* as well. And yet, once again, the Bible itself gives witness against this. St. John writes; "But there are also many other things which Jesus did; which, if they were written, every one, the world itself, I think, would not be able to contain the books that should be written" (John 21:25). He says, in addition: "Having more things to write unto you, I would not by paper and ink: for I hope that I shall be with you, and speak face to face: that your joy may be full" (2 John 1:12).

Yet this is still not enough for us. He for whom the Bible should be the source and guide of the Faith must also rationally be certain that it really is the Word of God. Now, my dear D., put your hand on your heart, and tell me what path you intend to take as a Protestant to arrive at such a certainty? The fact that parents, teachers and preachers have assured you of the divine inspiration of the Bible cannot be held to be sufficient for you, for here lies the path of personal authority, of oral transmission; the Catholic path, which you, as a Protestant, precisely must avoid on account of the principle of "the Bible alone."

Can reasons which are taken from miracles, the excellence of the teaching, the age and the authenticity of the Scriptures, the love of Truth of their authors, and so on serve you rationally? Aside from the fact that in this manner no certainty, but rather, in the best case, a greater or lesser degree of probability could be reached, and that only a small minority of men—the educated—could succeed in following such a path would also be thoroughly non-Protestant.

How about a feeling, "an inner voice," the "testimony of the Holy Ghost" in our breasts? But with this, "feeling" or "the inner voice" is openly put in the place of the Bible, which alone should decide the issue. Besides, modern Protestant criticism has already for a long time thoroughly rid itself of this fiction. Says Strauss in his *Glaubenslehre* (*Dogmatics*), "If it is an inner revelation of the Holy Ghost through which Holy Scripture is first recognized as being divine, it is therefore not the Scripture but precisely that inner knowledge of the Spirit that is the highest authority. With this, the most immeasurable subjectivism is raised to a principle." And further: "The other, more dangerous detour with which, on this point, the Protestant system oversteps itself is the rationalist one. If the inwardly perceived witness of the Spirit makes me certain of the divinity of Scripture, there is therefore need of only a limited reflection to bring up the further question of what assures me that this feeling that is in me comes from the influence of the Holy Ghost?" Reimarus, in his *Hamburg Fragmenten*, remarks: "The same inner witness which the Christian thinks he hears speak for the Bible speaks in Turkey for the Koran, offering a proof that this is only the specific common prejudice that each person has drunk with his own mother's milk."

And so the thinking Protestant who seeks to harmonize his Faith and his reason stands with the signpost "the Bible alone" before a clearly dark precipice. Where does it end? For most people, it ends with the abandonment of their Faith. Those who are not inclined to submit their reason to a Faith that does not appear to them to be a justifiable one do not find the path that could lead them to a rationally justified Faith. Who can count the host of souls who have already sunk into this abyss, and who would argue that it is only ignoble souls that have done so? I shudder at the thought of this mass damage, both of legions of individuals as well as the totality of men, who have grown up with and will still grow up with such a disastrously false principle!

One of the few who, while still on the pathway of independent examination, had the grace to discover not only the hollowness and nullity of Protestantism, but also the Truth in all of his fullness, the former Episcopal preacher Kent Stone, now a Catholic priest and member of a religious order, calls out to Protestants with respect to this, the point under contention:

> If you tell yourselves that the Bible must be inspired, when any uncertainty whatsoever comes to you regarding that inspiration, then your peace is destroyed. Your hope is based on your Faith and your Faith is based on the certainty of inspiration. The certainty of the inspiration however is based on—well, what? Your little world rests like that of the Hindus on an elephant, and the elephant rests on a turtle,

and the turtle, floats through the air. (Stone, *Invitation Heeded*, New York Catholic Publication Society, Second Edition, p. 140)

The already much cited P. von Hammerstein, also writes in his *Errinerungen* (pp. 52-53):

> Logic is only to be looked for in Catholicism and to some extent in complete disbelief denying all of Christianity. In disbelief, however, there lies only a logic that is one of total deception. Believing Protestantism, is a half measure; it is illogical to its innermost core and its deepest foundation. On the Catholic side, everything is based upon what is embodied and lives on Tradition, which gave us the Bible and tells us which of its books are correct, and which of them are inspired by God. On the Protestant side, Tradition is rejected as not being sufficiently reliable to support matters of Faith upon it; namely, insofar as it concerns the foundation of specific Catholic dogmas such as those of the Mass, Purgatory, the Ordination of priests, Extreme Unction and so forth.

> Should we seek to illustrate this approach vividly, we might make use of the following comparison. A man who has inhabited the first and second stories of his house in calm and peace for years hits suddenly upon the thought that a subterranean spring under the first story could undermine it and cause it to collapse. Full of concern for his life, the proprietor then inhabits only the second floor, without considering that if the story below caves in, the upper will dangle with great difficulty in mid-air.

> Let us now make the connection. The first story is Tradition, the second Holy Scripture, for this has solidity for us and counts as the Word of God only on the grounds of Tradition. The Protestants have declared the lower floor (Tradition) unreliable, but, despite this, build their whole religious structure on the second story, as though they were certain, without Tradition, to possess the Word of God

in these writings that on the grounds of Tradition were designated as Holy Scripture in the first place. Therefore they are in the same boat entirely as that man who seeks security in the second story when the first collapses. Or should we wish to make use of a shorter and more coarse proof, we could say: the Protestants saw off the branch on which they sit with Holy Scriptures.

The Bible is therefore neither clear, nor does it contain the full Word of God, nor can you as a Protestant be certain that it is the Word of God at all. And yet I am still not finished. Should you make use of the Bible alone as the source and norm of your Faith, then you must also be certain that the Bible that you have is the *genuine* Bible. Who vouches for that? Certainly not, the dead book itself that you hold in your hand marked with the title: "the Bible." There are also editions of the Bible in various languages, and even in one language there are different ones, with many passages read here in one way and there in another. Who tells you which edition is the correct one? Twist and turn as you may wish, you will not find a way out here either, without abandoning the Protestant groundwork. *Nolens volens* [whether you like it or not], you must confide in the authority of others: in Tradition, the Church Fathers, Councils and Popes, in an agreement with the Catholic past in order to be certain of the authenticity of your Bible.

Bossuet cries out to the Protestants, "You battle on the grounds of Holy Scripture and do not consider that this has come to us through Tradition." Luther himself admitted that fact, and indeed still did so in 1528: "It is true that God's Word and apostleship is to be found in Tradition, and we have taken Holy Scripture, Baptism, the Sacrament and the pulpit from it. What else could we have done?" (*Das IV. Cap. John. Durch D.M.L. gepredigt and ausgeleget*, Jena, 1568). Thus, you might have to ask "the Papacy" whether the book with the title "Bible" that you have in your hand is actually the correct Bible.

But the Papacy and the Roman Catholic Church were and are totally corrupt according to Lutheran teaching. More than this: they are not infallible, they can deceive you, and they can deceive themselves. You have to ascertain for yourself in a different manner what is genuine and what is false from the so-called Holy Scriptures—which Protestantism took over from the Papacy—in order to convince yourself of the authenticity or spuriousness of your own edition of the Bible as well.

You are also not permitted to rely on the authority of Luther, because this would mean vindicating Luther's infallibility, and that would be thoroughly un-Protestant. You must therefore proceed independently. To this end, you must be a perfect exegete.

> What is the authentic catalogue of the inspired books? Why did the Reformation eliminate the Books of Tobias and Judith and maintain the Book of Job? Why did it declare the Book of Wisdom, the Book of Ecclesiastes and the two last books of Maccabees to be apocryphal, while recognizing the Song of Solomon as being authentic?" You have to be a prominent linguist who knows Hebrew, Greek and Latin in order to test the accuracy of all translations, and indeed from the last of these to the first original texts. You must 'grasp the divine sense of the holy texts and gather all the articles of belief that they contain.' You must also be an experienced theologian, for you must "decide all of the controversies concerning Revelation definitively with the sole help of Scripture. (Causette, *Die Vernünftigkeit des Glaubens*, Mainz, Kirchheim, 1888, 403-404)

What requirements! But can they be avoided from the standpoint of the formal principle of Protestantism? They can by no means be avoided. They are an inexorable consequence of this. Is it necessary to develop the still further consequences? Supposing—I myself actually in no way concede this point— that some few out of the immeasurable mass of mankind would possess the time, the breath and the knowledge to come in this way to certainty, would they not become old and cold in doing so? Is Christianity really only a religion of old men? Does not a young man need a firm confession of Faith; indeed he, perhaps, all the more so than an old one? And if you succeed in reaching certainty in this way, what happens to your wife, your clerk, your gardener, your shoemaker, your maid, your laundress? Is the religion of Jesus Christ the monopoly of a small aristocracy of the mind? Did the Lord not say: "Let the Gospel be proclaimed to the poor?" Did he not choose poor fishermen as heralds of his teaching? Have not almost two hundred millions of uneducated people accepted his teaching and reached a certainty of Faith that even the cruelest death as a martyr would be incapable of shaking? Do not thousands of people who cannot even read still reach that certainty today in America, Africa, Asia and Australia?

Causette says:

> When I reflect that a rule of Faith must be understandable to all men, and the fewest number of these have the time and necessary knowledge to read the Holy Scriptures; that this rule must be easily applicable, because everyone, upon leaving childhood, should have a definitive Creed; that this Creed must not only remove every doubt but also all possibility of doubt, because in religious questions no doubt is allowed; then I wonder how it could be possible that on the grounds of such a logical hoax, one hundred fifty million men could still live cut off from the true Church.

Thus, it is possible to realize with crystal-clear clarity that the Bible alone cannot be the source of the Faith even while simply beginning a rational consideration of this question. But the reality of the problem becomes, if possible, still more evident from the contemplation of the impact that this false principle has had in the few centuries since the Reformation. What do we see when we consider it?

Already in Luther's lifetime the "Church of the Reformation" began to split, and this division has grown until our own time at a continually increasing pace. Look to your Germany. Where are your Lutherans today? They are a small minority, and even this minority is Lutheran in name only. No one shares Luther's dogmatic standpoint on all matters any longer. Says Kahnis, one among the many authorities dealing with the subject, "I ask that someone name me a dogmatic writing of a Lutheran theologian who on all points agrees with the original orthodox guiding concept." (*System der luth. Dogmatik*, 1868, p. IX). Then, next to the "Lutherans," you have your Unified Protestant Church, Reformed Church, and also even Baptists, Methodists and so forth.

If contemporary Protestantism in Germany does not yet display such a fissured picture as it does here in the United States, that is only thanks to the continuing influence of the authority of the State, which has worked from the outset for the protection and forcible spread of the Reformation's new form of church life. But even with this assistance, internal division could not be stopped. One man believes this; another, something different. And the mass of the population, especially the majority of the educated—the intellectual leaders—look upon the idea of Christ as folly. Who still thinks of ideals? Who still thirsts for the "Word that comes from the mouth of God?" Who still glows with noble enthusiasm for the True and the Good?

The great mass of the population, high and low, looks to its pleasures; it wants material possessions in order to enjoy itself. The better ones in its midst, those who feel that material things alone cannot quench the thirst for happiness which is innate in the human heart, look in vain for happiness in some lost little church in the woods of Vineta, the City of Wonders [a legendary city on the coast]. Meanwhile, an evil specter walks through the land, growing year by year—poverty and need. And those suffering from it are no longer humble and suppliant, but demand their rights with a scowl and with threatening fists. "Religion must be preserved among my people"; this is indeed a beautiful motto for princes. But in what way has it helped Germany; how will it continue to help?

Is the situation for religion with respect to Protestantism

better here, in the land of the free? People claim that this land is a genuinely Christian one, and the traveler who rushes quickly through our states and notices the innumerable churches and chapels and the Sabbath quiet on the Day of the Lord may easily be inclined to believe it. But the last census tells us that the majority of Protestants in the United States are not members of religious denominations, and whoever becomes more closely aware of the character of our hundredfold divided and scatterbrained sects knows that there is now bloody little of Christian substance to be found therein. Not a few of the German Protestants who came to this land turned to the Methodists and other sects, hundreds of thousands became lost in the sea of indifferentism and disbelief, and Lutheranism, almost the only Protestant religious denomination in the United States that still takes religion seriously, has at its command only a comparatively limited group of adherents and is, in addition, in no way dogmatically unified in itself.

What is it that the great mass of the almost one hundred thousand "Christian" sectarian preachers in America preach? They preach everything possible, but least of all the Bible that they allegedly place above all else. I recently saw in an American journal (*The Illustrated American*, New York, 1894, n. 21) a depiction of a "prominent" New York preacher, Dr. Parkhurst—who is now especially "*a la mode*"—in nine diverse poses. He sat, in the center, completely absorbed in the font of his inspiration—a newspaper. This picture is a thoroughly representative depiction of the American Protestant pulpit. It no longer culls its material from the Bible but instead has a penchant for the sensational daily Press.

Enough. Look wherever you wish within Protestantism, you will find in the place of a firm "*Credo*" a Babylonian confusion of fluctuating opinions, all in dispute with one another. The four words of Scripture "this is my body" had already in Bellarmine's day been subjected to two hundred different interpretations; Osiander verified twenty divergent views on Justification, and sixteen on Original Sin—all of them supposedly based upon

Holy Scripture—and this solely among those accepting the Augsburg Confession.

Today, this cacophony has become considerably more diverse. There are no longer any important Bible passages that are not interpreted by Protestant theologians and laity in a different way. The end will be chaotic, and there are Protestants themselves who see this drawing near as a consequence of the supposed principle of judgment upon "the Bible alone." One such observer writes in the *Nouvelliste Vaudois*:

> What is the actual principle of Protestantism? It is that of individual opinion in each and every religious question, in all of which the "I" makes himself the sole judge, tests everything, and creates his convictions. The conscience, taken as the criterion and starting point, is that "I" to the highest possible degree. Since among 'those people who actually examine questions' there are no two men who are in accord on all points, this unavoidably leads to the creation of individual churches. In the end, there must be as many church steeples as there are individual heads. That is the logical conclusion of Protestantism, which gains through individualism its providential "prize"— the dissolution of the Church into individual atoms being its necessary effect. But individualism is itself such a powerfully lacerating agent that after it has destroyed everything else, it must finally destroy itself.

And yet does the Bible itself not contain the admonition: "Search the Scriptures"? I feel that I can make sense of this admonition briefly on the basis of what has previously been said. I will answer with a counter-question: At the time that the Savior spoke those Words, was there already a Bible? No. As of yet, not a syllable of the New Testament had been written. The Lord was referring the Jews to whom he spoke to the writings of the Old Covenant so that they should recognize that these testified to Him as the coming Messiah.

I have, by now, my dear D., surely sufficiently substantiated to you the fact that the formal principle of Protestantism is indeed false. Protestant theologians also admit this, here and there, *nolens volens*. Thus, Kahnis writes: "A young theologian with good strengths and a solid ecclesiastical sense comes to the University. He naturally looks for a lodestar to guide his theological studies. This cannot be the Bible since all denominations and tendencies seek and find their teachings in it" (*Die Sache der luth. Kirche*, Leipzig, 1854, p. 45). This promising Protestant theologian then meets up with Tertullian, who tells him: "How useful can it be to invoke the Scriptures when one man asserts what the other denies?" ...But, Tertullian continues: "In order to know what Christ revealed to the Apostles, one has to turn to the Churches founded by him, to which they handed over their oral teaching along with their epistles." (*De Praescript.* C.,19). And so it is. For the Protestant who believes in Christ and has recognized the infirmity of Protestantism, there remains nothing else that he can do.

Your H.

~Chapter 14~
Popes & Papists, Popery & Poppycock

Dear D.,

You are right. The point to which our pathway has taken us will from now on be much more dangerous. For once a Protestant recognizes the total emptiness and groundlessness of the formal principle of Protestantism, he stands before a horrible dilemma. And who can say how many have already collapsed entirely in the face of it; as, for example, the Göttinger Professor Stäublin, who, upon realizing the folly of the formal principle of Protestantism, abandoned Christ and justified his abandonment with these words: "I must accept that if God had given a Revelation to men He would also have had to take care that the sense of that Revelation would not be handed over to the arbitrariness of subjective judgment. Jesus Christ's inconsistency in not having thought of this no longer permits me to see in him anything other than a benevolent wise man."

But, my dear D., today I fear for you no longer. You are indeed sure, as your letter, to my great joy, convinces me with increasing certainty, that God *has* given men a Revelation. Jesus Christ is, for you, the Son of God. You stand, once again, "firmly on the ground of the confession of the Apostolic Faith." Consequently, you have no doubt that we cannot speak, with Stäublin, of the "inconsistency of Jesus Christ." The God-Man must have taken sufficient care to ensure that his legacy to mankind would remain secure: in other words, that instead of the formal principle of Protestantism, invented by men, and recognized by us now as being false, there must be a true one, established by Christ the Lord Himself, by means of which everyone can be certain of all that they need to believe, with all doubt excluded. Indeed—and this completely eliminates all my concern for you—I see that you now also *pray* for such a certainty of Faith, and have formed the firm decision "to do, in consequence, what God wants." How could I still be anxious for your sake!

Well, then, let us admit that Christ founded a Church. We should hear this Church and we should accept her teaching. Christ equipped her, for this purpose, with full authority, and He identified her with unfailing, obvious "marks," so that everyone could easily recognize her as the Church founded by Him. But this Church is the Catholic Church. This is the truth that, with the help of God, I now want to prove to you.

Christ founded a Church—one Church. This divine foundation must therefore also be recognized through the unity reigning inside her. And it is the clearly expressed will of the Lord Himself that the world recognize the divinity of His foundation precisely on the grounds of the unity of the Apostles and all believers until the end of time. In His high priestly prayer he tells the Father: "And not for them [the Apostles] only do I pray, but also for them who through their word shall believe in me. That they all may be one, as thou, Father, in me, and I in thee; that they also may be one in us; that the world may believe that thou hast sent me" (John 17:20-21). The Apostle Paul also admonishes us to unity on this account, that all may be of one mind and one judgment without any kind of division. (1 Cor. 1:10). The Church of Christ must be one through the same Faith, the same grace, the same love and the same hope. (Ephesians 4:3-7).

Now, my dear D., everywhere you go in this wide world and wherever you find a Catholic place of worship, be it on the Tiber or on the Rhine, on the Mississippi or on the Congo, you will find precisely this unity: the same baptism, the same Faith, the same sacrifice, the same worship; and this among masters and servants, kings and beggars, learned and unlearned, black and white. Truly, that fact alone should be sufficient to prove that the Church in which hundreds of millions of the most diverse nations, races, classes, cultures and levels of education are united among themselves and in their relationship to Christ must be the Church of Christ.

But the miraculous unity of the Church is not exhausted with this fact. This unity is equally reflected in her constitution and organization.

The Lord compared the Church that He wished to found with a flock, with a kingdom, with a human body, with a house. His Church should therefore doubtless be an ordered whole. She should have a shepherd, a king, a head and a foundation. The Lord provided for this while He was still on earth. As long as He Himself visibly walked on the earth, *He* was the visible custodian and sustainer of the disciples living with Him; the center of unity Himself; king, shepherd, head, foundation, as He is today and will be for the whole Church until the end of time in an *invisible* manner.

However, before He withdrew from the eyes of the world, He chose Peter as the visible center of the Church on earth. Now, my dear D., this election is so clearly and certainly testified to in the Bible that after the grace of conversion was bestowed upon me it appeared incomprehensible to me how I had been able for so long to escape the overwhelming conclusiveness of this testimony. After Peter, first of all and alone among the Apostles, made a confession of his faith in Christ, the Lord said to him: "And I say to thee: That thou art Peter; and upon this rock I will build my church, and the gates of hell shall not prevail against it" (Matthew 16:18). But He said this to him after he had given to him, in place of his original name, the name of Peter. In light of this fact, which is as clear as day, the Protestant interpretation of the Lord's cited words as intending to declare "Himself" or "His preaching" as the foundation of the Church must appear to us to be downright childish.

Let us examine the question a bit further. Christ compares His Church with a house or a kingdom over which He has made Peter the Lord, by giving him the keys to it. "And I will give to thee the keys of the kingdom of heaven" (Matthew 16:19). He compares His Church to a flock of sheep and makes Peter its chief shepherd. "Feed my lambs, feed my sheep" (John 21:15-17). And the evening before His death He spoke to Peter: "Simon,

Simon, behold Satan hath desired to have you, that he may sift you as wheat: But I have prayed for thee, that thy faith fail not: and thou, being once converted, confirm thy brethren" (Luke 22:31-32). Peter was therefore meant to be the unshakeable foundation of the Church, her chief custodian; he who has to guard the whole flock, sheep and lambs; her infallible teacher of Faith.

And so the Bible clearly certifies for us that Christ the Lord honored Peter before all His Apostles and clothed him with the highest authority for His Church on the earth. However, that same Bible also just as clearly and definitively tells us that Peter actually *exercised* this authority. Hettinger summarizes these testimonies in a nutshell, with reference to the abundant sources of the Acts of the Apostles, as well as to Mark, Matthew, Peter and Paul, by saying:

> And so after the Ascension Peter arises first, completes the number of the Apostles and preaches to the people, works the first miracle, stands first before the Sanhedrin, holds the first Church visitation, and is the first who takes the gospel to the Gentiles in the wake of a special illumination. He is the chairman of the Council of Jerusalem, pronounces the excommunication of Simon, the first heretic, appears always first in the enumeration of the Apostles, and is expressly named as being the first. He confirms the writings of Paul, and Paul rushes off to see him in order to receive through him the seal of communion with the Church. (*Apologie*, III, p. 7)

But Christ had not founded His Church for the short lifetime of Peter alone, but for all time. The authority conferred upon Peter was conferred for the Church, for her maintenance in unity until the end of days, and therefore not attached to his person as such. If the kingdom, the flock, the body, the house of the Church were to persist after Peter's death, then the office of Peter had to continue. And it has continued since then, up until today, tied together with the See of the Bishop of Rome.

The fact that Peter was actually bishop in Rome is a truth historically so verified that even Protestant historical researchers today admit it. It is also a fact both that the Bishops of Rome have at all times considered themselves to be the successors of Peter and the bearers of his office of chief shepherd, as well as that no other bishop of the Catholic Church has contested this role. Moreover, all Catholic princes and peoples have always recognized the Bishop of Rome as the successor of Peter, as the visible Head of the Church, while everyone who has rejected the Supremacy of the Pope has always been considered by the totality of Catholics as an apostate.

This consensus, which has existed throughout all times and in the entire world, is a sufficient guarantee of the legitimacy of the Supremacy of the Roman See. But it is precisely because of this fact that those who oppose us have preferred to attack us as being Romanists, Papists and Ultramontanists. It is precisely because they know that this consensus exists, and that the object of this consensus—the supremacy of the Roman See—is the center of our unity, the link that holds us together in one flock, in one kingdom, in one body, in one visible Church, that they seek above all else to destroy the Papacy. If they could eliminate this consensus and separate us from our center, then their victory would be won. It is precisely also because of this that opponents make nothing in the Catholic Church more hateful to Protestants from their youth onwards than the pope, the "Antichrist." If this specter were not present, they would be deprived of the primary means of holding back those believing Protestants, to whom the hollowness and scatterbrained character of Protestantism is no longer hidden and who long for something better, from coming home to the Church of their fathers. I believe that you have arrived at a point where you can agree with me in this assertion.

We Protestants were taught—and I do not doubt that our good teachers themselves believed it—that the Rome usurped this supremacy, and that it originally did not exist. History teaches the opposite, but admittedly only to someone who has not limited himself to the study of non-Catholic works of history and turned instead to unadulterated sources. Already in the year 140 the then-reigning Pope, Sixtus I, could insist that no bishop who returned to his diocese from Rome without *littera formata*—that is to say without an Apostolic declaration that the Roman Pontiff had recognized that he was in communion with him—could be looked upon as being a legitimate bishop (H. W. Wouters, *Epoca*, II, 9). According to a citation of the Council of Chalcedon of 451, the Council of Nicaea, in 325, had already declared that: "The Roman Church always possessed the Primacy." The Council of Sardica in the year 347 wrote Pope Julius I that it was "in the highest degree suitable that the bishops of the Lord from all provinces conform with the Head, that is with the See of Peter." The Council of Chalcedon cited above called Pope Leo I "the highly blessed Apostle Peter, who is the rock and the foundation of the Catholic Church" after Dioscuros, Archbishop of Alexandria, had "dared to hold a Council without the authorization of the Apostolic See."

Authoritative testimonies of the same kind are found in the most ancient of the Church Fathers. St. Ignatius, who was a pupil of the Apostle, granted the Church of Rome the supremacy (*Epistle ad Rom.*, in subscription). St. Irenaeus, who taught only a little more than one hundred years after the death of Christ, wrote: "The whole Church, that is to say all believers in the world, must be in agreement with the Church of Rome with respect to principles. It is this Church that has received the Apostolic Tradition for the well-being of the whole world" (*Cont. Haeres.* I, III, n. 2). St. Cyprian (d. 258) called Rome the Seat of St. Peter and the sole "source of spiritual jurisdiction" (*Epistle. LV, ad Corn.*). Maximus (d. 335), Ambrose (397), Innocent I (417), Jerome (420) and Augustine (430) all spoke in the same way. The Papacy, therefore, was not usurped; it was not a work of men, but rather the work of God, created by Christ Himself, and, once again, as St. Thomas Aquinas said, "for the maintenance of unity." The Church has always recognized the Roman See as the seat of the highest authority, and she has always, in fact, exercised this authority.

When we are told that we place the pope on the same level as Christ, or even above Him, we can only respond to this with a compassionate smile. Compared to Christ, the pope, for us, is but dust, just as he himself indicates by calling himself merely the servant of His servants. The authority of the pope is great, but in comparison with the authority of Christ it is truly minimal—dependent, finite, limited. It is *from* Christ, but *under* Christ, and *for* Christ, and it is valid only for the Church on earth. The pope is a small, transitory part of the innumerable flock of Christ, that He, the eternal shepherd of our souls, will one day gather around Himself in that place where there will be no more need of a Deputy to maintain the flock in unity.

Incidentally, there is also no lack of Protestants who have defended us from foolish accusations generated by hate and spread by ignorance. For example, Leo, the renowned Professor of History, says this regarding one Rome-eating polemicist: "My opponent speaks of a Roman Catholic Church in which the authority of the pope counts for more than the authority of Christ, while I only know one in which the authority of the pope has a fixed purpose—to serve the light of Christ" (*Halle'sches Volkblatt*, 1852, n. 95).

Therefore, Christ founded a Church and established the Papacy as the center of her unity. However, grouped around this center, for the further safeguard of unity, stands a circle of clerics that is no less of divine appointment. For, according to the testimony of the Bible, the Lord while He walked upon the earth chose from among the crowd of those who believed in Him seventy-two disciples, and from among these, twelve Apostles to whom at diverse times and in the most clear and solemn manner He granted a special mission and task: "As the Father has sent me, so I send you" (John 6:58). "All power in Heaven and on earth is given to me. Go forth and teach all nations" (Matthew 28:18-19). "Teach all men to hold fast to all that I have commanded you" (Matthew 16:15). "Baptize all nations in the name of the Father, and of the Son, and of the Holy

Ghost" (Matthew 28:19). "He who hears you hears me, and he who despises you despises me" (Luke 10:16). "And whatsoever thou shalt bind upon earth, it shall be bound also in heaven: and whatsoever thou shalt loose on earth, it shall be loosed also in heaven" (Matthew 16:19). "Receive ye the Holy Ghost. Whose sins you shall forgive, they are forgiven them; and whose sins you shall retain, they are retained" (John 20:22-23).

These are words so crystal clear that there cannot arise even the shadow of a doubt concerning their meaning. Take them together with the equally clear words of the Lord to Peter and you have the appointment of a body that teaches, preaches the Gospel, baptizes, forgives or retains sins, rules by virtue of divine mission, and has at its summit a supreme bishop with whom each member, like the members of a body, must be bound together. You have here the hierarchy of my Catholic Church, with its pope, its bishops and its priests: that Church whose "magnificent constitution and unified organization" astounds her enemies, but against whose divine origin they struggle despairingly, since they would have to become Catholics were they to cease opposing her. Even the most bold illusionist could scarcely dare to conceive and maintain the thought that this amazing institution, untouched for almost two millennia through that storm tide of time which otherwise changes everything; this sole remaining point in the flood of all phenomena, could possibly be the work of men.

I will write to you next week regarding the other marks of the true Church. May God protect you!

Your H.

Chapter 15

Sinful Shepherds and their Unholy Catholic Church

Dear D.,

A further mark of the Church, the Bride of Jesus Christ, is her holiness. There is not the slightest doubt anywhere among Christians that the Church must be holy. Even you confess a belief in a holy Church. However, if we now want successfully to investigate whether the mark of holiness is really to be found in the Catholic Church, we must be clear before all else what, exactly, the concept of holiness is all about.

Holiness can be something objective or subjective. Objectively, all Christians gain holiness by means of Holy Baptism. Through this, they are consecrated to God and called to sanctification. Obviously, our present investigation is not concerned with holiness in this sense. For how could we distinguish the Church of Christ among all the hundreds of faith communities of Christian name in this manner? We are concerned here with visible, unmistakable characteristics; with subjective holiness; with the heroic love of God and neighbor, as well as with the reality of those higher, supernatural gifts through which Christ wanted to identify His Church before the whole world.

As we look around to see where we find these marks, we must protect ourselves from one serious error; namely the one that would focus our argument only or even only primarily on persons. This error would lead us solely or primarily to make a comparison between persons inside and outside of the Church. The apologist, Causette, whom I cited earlier, speaks correctly of the holiness of the Church when he says:

> God save me from turning the present thesis into a question of persons, confronting Catholics and dissidents

and then ascribing all the virtues to the one and all the vices to the other. For I very well know that we have brothers among believing heretics and schismatics who bear the marks of evangelical grandeur and Christian beauty, and that it would be unjust to be mistaken about this, sacrilegiously and cruelly judging those whom God has decided to save. (Causette, *Vernünftigkeit des Glaubens*, p. 494)

In order to recognize the holiness of the Catholic Church, we must first, above all else, look towards her doctrines with respect both to faith and morals, seeing whether these are fit to sanctify those who follow them. Now, my dear friend, it is the Catholic Church, and she alone, that demands sanctification from her children. "Be ye perfect, as your heavenly Father is perfect," Jesus admonishes His disciples in the Sermon on the Mount (Matthew 5:48). The Church says exactly the same thing to her children. She seeks to have her children invigorated with a true love for Christian perfection from earliest youth onwards, guiding them to the exercise of all virtues, to abhorrence of all sins, and to true compliance with all divine commands.

For this purpose, she urges a diligent and persistent use of the means of grace, above all those of prayer and the Holy Sacraments. She exhorts us to works of spiritual and corporal mercy insofar as our other duties permit us to undertake them. She calls on us to instruct the ignorant, to come to the help of those in danger, to support the poor, and lovingly to embrace the sick, the orphaned, the helpless aged and the imprisoned; to bury the dead and to pray for their poor souls; to assist the living with our intercessions. In order to sanctify us, the Church continually places the love of Jesus Christ before our eyes as the most complete model of perfection, and, after this, the holy lives of those who practiced in heroic measure the virtues of humility, obedience, chastity, meekness, patience, self-denial, piety, persistence and zeal. For words move us, and examples pull us strongly towards imitation. The Church commands us ceaselessly to watch and to pray, so as not to stain our souls even for a moment, be this only through an evil thought. She lovingly pursues those who have had the misfortune of going astray and encourages them through contrition and penance to turn back onto the right path and to purge their stained souls in the blood of the lamb.

She forbids even the most simple of injustices against our neighbors, whether they be friend or foe, Christian, Jew or Pagan, and she obliges us in the most severe way to repair, as far as possible, any injustice that we have committed, making up for any damages inflicted. While forbidding injustice, she also demands from us everything that God has commanded, encouraging us to practice those highest virtues whose observation Jesus Christ did not prescribe but rather only advised. These are the so-called Evangelical Counsels: abandonment of the world and all of its charms by following Christ alone in poverty, chastity and obedience. Truly, the mark of holiness of the Catholic Church as an institution is so clearly stamped upon her teachings that no one who searches for it with good will can mistake it.

Secondly, we would also like to enter into an investigation of the fruits that the holiness of the teaching Church has brought forth and still brings forth among the men who listen to her message. There is no doubt on the part of those knowledgeable of history that it was the Catholic Church that renewed the face of a world sunk deeply in sins and vices in the first centuries of her existence. The holiness of the Christians was a revelation to their pagan contemporaries: "See how they love one another!" they cried out in astonishment. The multitudes of those who sealed the Gospel with their blood pass through the first three centuries of the Church like the myriad of stars of the Milky Way in the firmament; among them are found more than thirty popes. And although this stream never poured out in such abundance again, it does still flow down to our own day.

Name for me a land in Christendom whose soil is not saturated with the blood of Catholic martyrs. Who was it who rescued our pagan forefathers in Germany from barbarism? It was those heroes of Christian missionary zeal; a Boniface and a Willibrord, a Corbinian, a Rupert, and all the rest. Protestants speak of them with reverence as well. Were they perhaps Lutherans or Calvinists? Who is it, still today, who are the pathfinders of the Christian mission if not Catholic priests, and how many of them continue in the present century, even up until our own day, to crown the work of their selfless holy devotion with a martyr's death?

Truly, the Catholic Church not only was the fruitful mother of saints, but *still is*, and the convert Stone (now Father Fidelis) well indicates the experience of many other converts when he writes in the book we have already cited (*The Invitation Heeded*, pp. 197, 198).

> I looked back {as a believing Protestant) with melancholy to that distant, glorious time when virtues grew to mammoth proportions and the fire of devotion glowed in a clear blaze. I knew that there were giants then. Their heroic forms rose up from the golden perfume of the past before me. I thought of our own dwarf-like age, of the cold, calculating, penny-pinching piety of the present, and the words of the pagan poet came to my mind: *Hos utinam inter heroas natum tellus me prima tulisset!* [if only the early ages had given me birth to be among such heroes as these! Horace, *Satires* 2.2]
>
> Oh, the indescribable joy that soared in me when I first began to study the life and the writings of the Catholic saints of recent times! The New World could not have risen before the eyes of the Genovese discoverer more gloriously than these islands of the blessed did before me. Here lay the inexhaustible sources of bliss that that I dreamed of in the remote past. Here was the race of the saints that I presumed had long died out. Oh, holy Church! O fruitful mother, who, while men called you withered, had as children an Ignatius, a Francis Xavier, a Charles Borromeo, a Theresa, an Aloysius, a Philip Neri; who later suckled a Francis de Sales and a Vincent de Paul and gave to us almost in our

own day an Alphonsus Liguori and Paul of the Cross!

Even some Protestants cannot close their eyes to the fact that the tree of the Catholic Church is much richer in the fruits of sanctity—*sit venia verbo* [pardon my saying so]—than the tiny one growing in the garden of Protestantism. Here and there, they have even dared to admit this openly. Hence, Victor A. Huber:

> In speaking about Roman Catholicism, we can confidently assert, both from our own experience, as well as from other sources, that the works of Christian benevolence performed therein in a consciously ecclesiastical and Christian spirit, both organizationally and personally, are present in far more magnificent, abundant and diverse forms than on our part.

> This is particularly valid for France, a country that what we, with so little sense of fairness, experience and self-judgment, love to treat as though she were the model of every national and conservative expression of listlessness... What is at work there, above all else, is the expression of freely offered personal works of love. We find over thirty thousand nuns and almost just as many brothers engaged in active, charitable works of incomparable self-sacrifice. Yes, they are indeed bound, in part, by their vows of obedience, poverty and chastity, but they took these vows voluntarily. Any tourist who has examined their works of love in an unbiased spirit would agree with us when we claim that the mere sight of the habit of those charitable nuns already makes a beneficial, calming impression both upon those who are suffering as well as the onlooker.

> What is at work here is actually the fulfillment of the calling to Christian and feminine charity. One finds in France more than ten times as many thousands of those answering this call as here [among German Protestants] ...In our observation of these activities in Roman lands we have never sensed the lack of a full and direct outpouring

of truly human or evangelical love. It seems as though it would be more worthy of those truly dedicated to pure doctrine to be driven by the sight of such an example to a more rigorous self-judgment. (*Inner Mission*, 1864, p. 117)

One man who has very little to do either with Catholicism or Protestantism, and who generally vilifies and persecutes both of them with a downright diabolical ferocity, writes: "Those who have split off from the Roman Communion practice Christian love of neighbor only incompletely. There is perhaps nothing more grand to see on this earth than the sacrifice made by members of the tender sex, with their beauty, youth, and often their illustrious birth, soothing human suffering in hospitals despite all of those horrors, the sight of which are so mortifying to our pride and so appalling to our weakness." It is Voltaire who said this, a man who adequately proclaimed his hatred for the Church through his famous slogan: "*écrasez l'infâme*" [crush the loathsome thing] (*Sur les moeurs*, III, p 139). Similar avowals of Protestants and unbelievers can be compiled in volumes.

The Catholic Church is therefore holy, not only as an institution through her teachings, her regulations, her remedies and her activities, but also because she constantly brings forth rich fruits of her sanctity in those who belong to her.

But if there was a Judas already to be found among the Twelve whom Christ the Lord Himself had chosen as His disciples—men who were direct witnesses of His holy life, His holy teaching, and His miracles—should it surprise us that also later, even in our own time, imperfect, weak and really evil men, even in His Church, are to be found among those who bear His Name? And this all the more frequently when in one place or another circumstances tend to favor corruption?

Before I became a Catholic, a venerable old priest, whom I sometimes met to discuss controversial questions, said to me, often highlighting the point that he was making, "Dear friend, men do what men do everywhere." I have to confess that at the time I did not fully understand what he meant. I soon came to grasp its meaning, and I am still thankful for what he then told me. (I think that priests instructing converts, especially in the United States, never pass over this point fleetingly; in fact, under certain circumstances, they are used to emphasizing it quite firmly and clearly, particularly when dealing with idealists).

I was a Catholic for scarcely a few months when another convert looked me up and recited to me a long tale of woe regarding murky experiences that he had had with various Catholics, including priests and prelates. I tried to show him the wrongheadedness of the consequences that he wished to draw from them—for himself and perhaps also for me—with respect to the Catholic Church. I assured him that his tales could not change my conviction one iota, not even if they were a thousand times worse. The Church on earth is composed of men and "men do what men do everywhere." But I soon noticed that the unfortunate man had already fallen away from the Faith inwardly. He later committed suicide. Nevertheless he had had the grace, while still at his hour of death, to turn once again to the Church—as I hope, to save his soul, although only "as through fire."

Another convert wrote me about his trip to Rome. He also did not find everything there to be precisely as he had desired, and, in fact, had experienced quite a number of disappointments among Catholics in other locations as well. He had only found the warm, helpful sympathy that he felt entitled to receive from Catholics among a few noble souls, despite the many great sacrifices that he had made in converting, and his consequent dependence upon them now for almost everything. He remained for years, and this despite his great learning and talent as an author, without a position and a fixed home, scarcely able to buy bread for himself and his family with the pen that finally, today, has procured for him a widely respected name.

Still, these experiences did not tempt him to lose his Faith at all, because he was a genuine and totally convinced believer. "Men do what men do everywhere," even among those who call themselves Catholics, and even when one understands that "doing what men do everywhere" also means that these Catholics also give in to their human weaknesses and imperfections. Catholics occasionally "do what men do everywhere" among themselves even to a greater degree than they do among those who believe differently. I myself have often noticed this truth, to my very great sorrow. At times like those, one really feels like swiftly pulling out a sword, as Peter did when the Lord was betrayed and taken prisoner. But when that temptation strikes, it is better to aim one's eyes inwardly to ascertain whether or not there is a slice of his own flesh that has need of that swift, cutting sword; whether one himself is really certain that he would not, like Peter, despicably deny the Lord that he momentarily felt himself to be oh so ready to defend.

"Men do what men do everywhere," and we ourselves do as well. But if the Catholic man that "does what men do everywhere" is allowed to develop his tendencies unchecked, he will generally be worse than a non-Catholic who has abandoned things divine, and he will be infinitely worse than a man who is a *bona fide* but faithful Protestant. How could it be otherwise? A Catholic knows the Truth, completely and fully; he knows each and every thing that God wants from him, and he also has the means of helping him to fulfill the will of the Lord in the Church. *Corruptio optimi pessima* [the corruption of the best is the worst] That is already an old saying. The higher someone stands, the harder and deeper he can fall.

Therefore, "men do what they do everywhere," also in the Church, the temporal Church, composed of quarrelsome creatures. Men have "done what men do everywhere" inside the Church more or less from the outset, and the same will be true until the end of time. There are, were and will be abuses, offenses, Judases, at all times. And there are times in which these defects, abuses, offenses and Judases will so proliferate in individual parts of the enormous kingdom of the Church that that entire kingdom will seem to be threatened. It was like this, for example, in our own Fatherland at the time of the "Reformation." Despite the epoch-making researches of Janssen, it cannot be denied that the Catholic Church of Germany in the sixteenth century displayed many serious defects. If it had not been so, the massive abandonment of the Church by Germans in the age of the "Reformation" would be inexplicable. And it has often been like this during the almost nineteen centuries of the history of the Church.

But let no one be misled regarding this fact. Christ the Lord Himself predicted it. He said that offenses must come; adding, as He who would return to judge all things, the words "woe to those through from whom they come!" And thrice woe to those from whom they come if they have a high position in the Church on earth! Climb down into Hell with that outspoken Catholic author of the *Divina Commedia* and you will find bearers of the tiara and the miter who have defiled their holy office due to simony, enduring the appalling eternal pains of the "third circle," their heads crammed downwards into the blazing lake of fire. One day, that frightful *dies irae*, the "court of the world" will judge everything that has been done, with punishments thrice more terrible for those "hirelings" and "wolves in sheep's clothing" who were treated here on earth as "venerable" and "most venerable," even though the term "base" would have been more suitable to describe their person. "*Judicabit judices judex generalis. Ibi nihil produit dignitas papalis. Sive sit episcopus, sive cardinalis, Reus condemnabitur, nec quaretur qualis*" [The general judge will judge the judges; there the papal dignity will in no way help; be he bishop, be he cardinal, the guilty one will be condemned, nothing will be hidden or have to be investigated].

This question also has another side to it that will certainly astonish you, but whose meaning, if you consider it correctly, can scarcely remain unacknowledged. Montaigne recounts the tale of a visitor from the time of Alexander VI "who, intending to go to Rome to admire the holiness of our morals, and who, after having seen the corruption of the contemporary prelates and people, clung all the more firmly to our religion because he said to himself that only a divine power could maintain it in such profane hands." In fact, that man was correct. Whoever surveys the history of the Church and pictures the thousands of dangers that have threatened her and still threaten her with downfall not only from the outside but also from the inside— from men Catholic in name; whoever looks upon this vast, majestic cathedral that has been built on the rock of Peter from out of that small Pentecost congregation in Jerusalem, extending its foundation farther today than ever before throughout all parts of the earth, beyond all the seas, despite all such dangers; whoever does this, cannot escape the conviction that someone higher than man has built and has held His hand defensively over His work.

When and where "men do what men do everywhere" among members of the Catholic Church, this always happens *despite* the Church. It happens because the teachings and the regulations of the Church are disobeyed. For these teachings and regulations are holy and, where they are followed, they can only bring forth sanctity and saints.

It is the other way around with Protestantism. Does Protestantism as such have a teaching that forms saints? Perhaps through its teaching of the enslavement of the human will, of man's complete incapability of doing what is good? Or the teaching that there is only one true virtue and one true vice— faith and disbelief—and that good works are not only useless to eternal salvation but even harmful? Would not such teachings have to nip all serious striving for Christian perfection in the bud? I well know that there are those today who call themselves Lutherans who no longer want to acknowledge such teachings. And yet they *are* genuine teachings of Luther, found again and again in the work of the so-called Reformer, who also distorted the Sacrament of Marriage, that foundation of the entire social order, transforming it into "a purely earthly thing" and "allowing" two wives to Philip of Hesse, as recent Lutheran authors, thanks to Janssen, themselves now concede (See the *Conservative Monatsschrift*, March, 1883).

How can one wonder that that science of Moral Theology

that has a place in the Church next to that of Dogmatic Theology and was nurtured by the best Christian spirits from the time of the Fathers onwards has completely withered away in Protestantism? There are not lacking some recent Protestant theologians who very well understand this glaring shortcoming of Protestantism and find it painful. Heinrich Thiersch admits:

> After all, they [some among those of the so-called Reformers] abandoned the belief in the real possibility of the sanctification of men. Because they took ordinary human practice as the sole measure of what was attainable, they displaced the goal to be put before the Christian. This goal was called perfection. Actually, the Reformers did not attribute to the Faith too much power; they attributed to it too little. Let us rely on Christ for this as well: He gave us the victory over sins and the power to achieve true sanctity. The weakness of the old, original Protestantism is shown in its dubious conception of sanctity. This weakness displays its adverse influence on all sides. (*Überschriftl Familienleben*, Frankfurt, 1857, p. 18)

Nevertheless, if there are also among Protestants souls that are noble and holy, they are there *in spite* of Protestant teachings, confess these teachings with their mouths and zealously champion them all that they may like. What actually ennobles them is the possession of an *anima naturaliter Christiana* [a naturally Christian soul], thanks to the influence of the Church that remains effective even on the opposite side of the denominational fence, binding inwardly to her life what is cut off from her externally.

Warm regards, H.

~Chapter 16~
Miracles: No Such Thing!

My Dear D.,

Another mark of the true Church that is in harmony with the mark of sanctity is the gift of miracles. God has always made the men to whom He has given special tasks for the salvation of mankind recognizable by granting them the gift of miracles; or, more accurately, He has performed miracles though them; undeniable miracles, as clear as day. How else did the people unmistakably recognize Moses and the Prophets, already in the days of the Old Covenant, as being men of God? By nothing other than the miracles worked by them though the power of God. The people saw this and on account of this listened to them as messengers of Jehovah.

Similarly, Christ the Lord attested to His own mission through miracles. He Himself said: "But I have a greater testimony than that of John [the Baptist]: for the works which the Father hath given me to perfect, the works themselves which I do, give testimony of me, that the Father hath sent me" (John 5:36). And, another time, He said: "Though you will not believe me, believe the works" (John 10:38). Furthermore, when John the Baptist, who was in prison, had two of his disciples ask whether He were the promised Messiah, He referred them to the "works" that He had just done. "And Jesus making answer said to them: Go and relate to John what you have heard and seen. The blind see, the lame walk, the lepers are cleansed, the deaf hear, the dead rise again" (Matthew 11:4-5).

As the Lord Himself, His Church also, after His return to the Father, also displayed the gift of miracles, this unmistakable seal of divine mission. He clearly and explicitly foretold her possession of this gift in the solemn moments before His Ascension. Hence, he said to His Apostles: "Go forth in the whole world and preach the Gospel to all creatures." And then

133

He continued: "And these signs shall follow them that believe: In my name they shall cast out devils. They shall speak with new tongues. They shall take up serpents: and if they shall drink any deadly thing, it shall not hurt them. They shall lay their hand upon the sick: and they shall recover" (Mark 16:17-18.) Accordingly, what could be more certain than the fact that the true Church would also be recognized through possession of the gift of miracles?

Now, is this gift found in Protestantism? Let us go back to its origins. Did Luther perhaps work miracles? One might reasonably expect this from a man who held himself up as a reformer of the Church who had been sent from God. But one finds no belief from the millions of Christians who heard his word that he proved his divine calling to those doubting him by means of miracles. But when others began to "reform," Luther most emphatically demanded such a proof from them. Hence, he reproached his earlier friend, Karlstadt, with "peddling his stuff without being called." He said, "God does not break down an old order and establish a new one without great signs being involved." And again: "Whoever brings something new onto the track or wants to teach something different must be called by God and strengthen the proof of his calling with true miracles. He should hit the road if he cannot pull this off" (Waich, *L.W.*, IX, p. 1009).

He himself had no such verification of his divine mission. Nevertheless, he dared to demand unlimited belief in his word by saying that: "whoever does not recognize my teaching does not want to be saved; for this teaching is God's, not mine; and therefor my court is that of God, not mine" (*Erl. Ausg.* 28, 144). Yes, he dared to damn the opponents of his teaching for all eternity: they "should have hell fire on their heads and no thanks in the bargain. That is my, Doctor Luther's answer from the Holy Ghost and the true Holy Gospel" (*Erl. Ausg.*, 25, 76). Luther presumed to do with innumerable millions what the entire Church never does and never can do even to one single soul: deny them eternal salvation. He placed himself on the chair of the eternal judge; he, a creature born of dust like you and me; a creature whom his disciples themselves have long admitted was not a saint and did not work miracles.

Did God perhaps later, after Luther's death, strengthen through miracles the "Church of the Reformation" or any of the innumerable sects, big and small, into which this has since then splintered? I have endeavored in vain to uncover any such miracles in Protestantism.In any case, I have heard it said by teachers and preachers from my early youth onwards that the days of signs and wonders were absolutely long gone anyway; that such things happened and were only necessary for Christ Himself and perhaps still for the times of the Apostles.

Indeed, I have heard and read from others that there are no miracles at all; that one does not need to believe the biblical miracles themselves; and even so one can still be a Christian. Millions of Protestants have adopted this latter standpoint for a long time already. But it should be clear to anyone who knows Holy Scripture even only superficially that in believing such a thing, the credibility of Holy Scripture, the truthfulness of Christ, and with this, not only His divinity but also His sanctity are denied. The authors of Holy Scripture are thereby stamped as being liars and Christ as a swindler.

Liberal Protestant theology is magnificently identified in a collection of sermons (or rather, a collection of "religious talks") published by the Clerical Inspector of the Seminary in Magdeburg, Professor Bornemann. Yes, Dr. Bornemann still calls Christ the Redeemer. Nevertheless, he denies His divinity as well as His miracles. He preaches of the healing of the deaf and dumb man, but construes it in the following manner: "This healing in and of itself has no meaning for us; only for the man who is healed and for his relatives." In fact, it is "totally indifferent" to us, and it is for this reason that Christ forbade speaking of it. He also thinks that Christ was not omnipotent, for "everything that He does by way of healing points not to His own but to divine omnipotence, and to His own love of redemption." He does not reveal what the miracle actually is all about. He admits that "certain persons" had a "certain power." But he could not suddenly give speech and hearing to the deaf and dumb. It is for this reason that we have Institutes to deal with such people!

The conclusion of this curious "sermon" reads: "We do not need to be in agreement in particulars over our textual history; one man clarifies it in one way; another in a different manner." What a sad blindness! The truth is that neither "the one" nor "the other" "clarifies" anything whatsoever. Rather, we "let the textual history rest where it is"—thoughtless. And despite his denial of miracles and of Christ, by means of this subterfuge the dimwit claims that he still remains a Christian, living out his Faith obtusely.

But why do I speak of this! I do not need to talk you out of this "standpoint" any longer, although I do need to speak of the other theme: that miracles count among the things that "have been" but of which we no longer have any need at all. Now, my dear D., this is, as Dr. Fabri, the Director of Missions of Barmen, himself a Protestant, has seen and admitted, nothing other than a stopgap standpoint, a "conventional mode of speaking, by means of which our [Protestant] stupidity and our constant lack of the powers and gifts of the Spirit, has been clothed, as with a fig leaf."

Dr. Fabri continues,

> It is indeed peculiar that Holy Scripture does not offer the slightest evidence for this subterfuge; rather, the opposite confronts the unbiased reader everywhere....We openly confess that we have never had the heart confidently to excuse our shortcomings in dealing with this question and in comparing it with the traditional view; to excuse our groaning for a more complete manifestation of the Spirit and our recognition of the power of the subterfuge suffocating it; to silence our longing for this more powerful proof of the Holy Ghost through miracles. (*Die Neuesten Erweckungen*, Barmen, 1860, p. 50ff)

This is very true. And not a few other Protestants have made the same point with different words: that miracles must continue in the true Church of Christ, but that Protestantism cannot be shown to offer them. How curious however that they leave it at that and continue to remain Protestants! If they were logical, they would have to conclude that the Church of Christ could not be in Protestantism; that she must consequently be outside of it. But admittedly, they would then once more stand at the gates of Rome. And Truth simply cannot be *there*; that would be impossible to contemplate from the very outset.

Now, let us see. Holy Scripture attests to the fact that in the days of the Apostles, the preaching of the Gospel of God was confirmed by the miracles that followed upon it, and believing Protestants also do not deny this. But what can we say about miracles of later times? An unbroken chain of witnesses extends through all the centuries indicating that God again and again made His Church recognizable and glorified her through miracles. First there are the Fathers and teachers of the Church who testify to this reality. Irenaeus, Basil, Athanasius, Jerome, Chrysostom, Ambrose, Augustine and others appeal for acceptance of the truth and divinity of their teaching to the gift of miracles that they themselves and other saints of their time performed; miracles that were missing to those teaching error. In later centuries, St. Bernard, St. Dominic and St. Francis Xavier did the same. Many Protestants call upon these witnesses with great respect.

Sadly, however, Protestant arbitrariness and illogic once again show themselves here as well. On the one hand, these saints are held to be men of God, while on the other, Protestants either do not believe or unceremoniously declare all of their words that testify for the Church and against Protestantism to be subsequent falsifications. Admittedly, they cannot prove this, but that is understandable because otherwise it would once again be a story of their having to become Catholic.

Today as well, even in our own times, witness is borne to the fact that the hand of the Lord has not yet been taken away from the Catholic Church. How often have you yourself read that a canonization has once again taken place in Rome? Naturally, you have smiled upon hearing this; perhaps you have also felt a little quiet outrage with respect to this "blasphemous hocus-pocus" that the great "Dalai Lama" of the "Papists" allowed himself to perform once again. Did I not do the same? Sadly, yes. We were superior to such "unreasonable demands on the credulity of backward spirits"; we knew better; we had heard and read "how this is done." Once again a new "lie-legend," as we called it, had been coined. We pitied the poor "dumb sheep in the Roman sheep pen" and enjoyed "all the more our own superiority." We were endlessly clever and wise; clever and wise like someone who did not know his own mother, but now willingly condemned her in accord with the gossip of chatterboxes who likewise never had any knowledge of the poor woman.

It is well known to the Catholic that proof is demanded for every canonization, especially when this does not concern a martyr; that many miracles have already taken place through the invocation of the saint in question. It is also well known to Catholics that the proving of the potential saint's miracles is undertaken with painful accuracy; that the proofs must be above any and all doubt before they are considered to be valid. No court of justice of the world can go to work on its cases more thoroughly and carefully than that tribunal of those learned men, with a special reputation for integrity, most of them of a venerable age—already close to appearing before their own Judge—to whom the guidance of the process of canonization falls due. The investigation is often repeated two or three times; it employs for its purposes a man of especially excellent theological and juridical formation who seeks critically to rebut the proofs brought before the court. Furthermore, before a miracle is recognized as such learned natural scientists and physicians are questioned for their expert opinions as to whether the incident in question perhaps might not have happened in a natural manner. And in this way, the tribunal often continues its examination for long years before it makes its judgment even only over a few facts.

The following episode testifies to just how accurately this tribunal deals with the proof of miracles. An English Protestant in Rome expressed doubt about the procedure to a cardinal with whom he was friendly. The cardinal allowed him an examination of a cross section of records that contained the usual proceedings concerning different miracles. The Englishman read through these attentively and afterwards confessed to the cardinal: If all miracles were as clearly proven as these had been, then he must give in and admit his error in doubting the tribunal. How astonished must he have been when he received as an answer: "And yet none of these proofs were recognized as being sufficient!"

Apart from that, the Church is not satisfied just to exert the utmost care in such matters; she also warns her children against giving faith to all apparently supernatural incidents without any further ado, and seriously confronts abuses in this realm. We had a case of this sort just recently in our vicinity, in the Diocese of Winona in Minnesota. A painting of the Mother of God was said to have appeared in a supernatural manner in the window of a little village Catholic Church. Protestant newspapers reported this at large, and the supposedly miraculous cures that were said to have occurred there as well. It is no wonder that due to the dissemination of this somewhat highly hopeful-sounding report, a handful of Catholics gradually were induced to visit the place, and some of them believed in the "miracle." Nevertheless, the Catholic Press and the Catholic clergy behaved extremely cautiously. It was the bishop of that diocese who finally after a short investigation put an end to the sensation which had arisen either from credulity or the self-interest of some individual.

However, no rational person would doubt the fact that miraculous phenomena, miraculous healings and answers to prayers, in reality still do take place in the Catholic Church as they have from time immemorial, if he familiarized himself with the history of Lourdes, of Catherine Emmerich, of Louise Lateau, or that of the latest exposition of the Holy Coat of Trier.

Admittedly, it is again not sufficient to get a true picture of these histories by merely hearing what opponents and enemies of the Church, or those who hold the very idea of miracles to be folly from the outset, have to say about them.

For example, after you, to your satisfaction, have "come to know of" the "amazing journey to see the Holy Coat"—doubtless from Protestant and Jewish newspapers—read the book of Bishop Korum, *Miracle and Divine Favors at the Exposition of the Holy Coat in Trier in the Year 1891, as Presented by the Documents*, that was recently released by the firm of the Paulinus Publishing House in Trier as well. You will then easily recognize that these matters actually possess a more serious side to them than that which has been speciously offered to you. This book presents eleven cases of cures that, according to expert medical opinions, cannot be explained in any natural way. They represent, in consequence, without a doubt, a direct intervention of God. It also speaks of a rather large number of other cures alongside these, in which most readers will equally hold a natural explanation as being excluded. But the Church authorities did not recognize the proof of a miracle as having been demonstrated in their cases.

Although the Church goes about judging such matters with extreme precision, she nevertheless in no way demands from her children absolute belief in any of the miracles examined by her. And yet, if historical facts are in any way demonstrable at all, then these are the ones that are—so much so that those who are not intellectual philistines from Berlin and Parisian arts page columnists might rely on them.

Yes, I dare to make the assertion that the more fertile the spirit of those who approach an examination of the Church with good will, the more they are equipped with education and knowledge, the easier they will recognize that the latter in truth is the Church of Jesus Christ, because next to the other marks thereof, she very clearly bears that of the gift of miracles.

God be with you! Your H.

~Chapter 17~
Christianity Is Not the Catholic Church

My Dear D.,

Jesus Christ sent his Apostles out into the whole world, to all nations. His Church should, therefore, be a general, Catholic one. If you believe that, you cannot possibly believe that your "National Church"—this drop in the sea of Christendom, the very name of which is unknown to millions of Christians several dozen miles past your border—or any other so-called Church which is limited to one or a few countries, to one or to but a few nations, can be the Christian Church.

Here, therefore, we have a further mark of the true Church: her catholicity. And, truly, whoever looks for the Church on this basis cannot err.

But there is such a Church that actually does really dare to make the claim to be the Catholic Church, the whole Church, the Church as such, while all the remaining truly or supposedly Christian denominations only consider themselves to be parts or branches of that Church. And this one Church is actually Catholic, spread throughout all lands and nations and parts of the globe, in full unity of Faith, hope and love, despite all the differences of language and culture; a universal Kingdom of the Spirit, led by one Spirit.

St. Augustine already wrote,

> What keeps me firmly in the Catholic Church is the unity of peoples and nations, the authority founded upon miracles, nurtured through hope, propagated in love, and fortified through its antiquity. The succession of bishops up until the present episcopacy, starting with the See of Peter to which the Lord Himself entrusted the pasturing of His sheep after His Resurrection, also keeps me firmly in her fold. Finally, the name Catholic holds me fast, and

it is not without reason that it is this Church alone, among so many heresies, that possesses that name.Although all heretics want to be called Catholic, should a stranger ask how to get to the Catholic Church, not one of them would dare to point out to him his own basilica or his own house. (*C. duas Ep. Pelag.* I, 14)

Yes, the Church of Christ then fully possessed and still fully possesses today the name Catholic. Not only has she everywhere made and continues to make a claim to this name, but this was and will always and everywhere be conceded to her.

And yet perhaps you will say: "What is in a name? Many things bear a name in the world that is not owed to them. Consequently the mere name is no necessarily accurate characterization." Not so, my friend. The name with which an individual, a party, an age or a thing is designated certainly can mislead and does do so very often. Thus many today call "liberal" what others hold to be the opposite.

But this is not what is involved here. It is not an individual, a party, an age, which attributes to this Church the name Catholic but the *sensus communis* through all times and lands. It is precisely this same *sensus communis* that has given testimony on her behalf, and that has never renounced it to direct it elsewhere. Heretics and schismatics of all times have borne the brunt of this testimony and have taken all imaginable efforts to destroy it in consequence. And yet they have not succeeded.

Already Gregory of Tours says that the Arians stubbornly called the Catholics "Romans," and yet the Arian heresy, like so many others, has vanished, and the name "Catholic" has remained with the Church afterwards as beforehand. Similarly, Protestant preachers, writers and publicists have tried just as stubbornly for three hundred seventy years to wrest the name Catholic from the Church of Christ by calling this the "Roman Church" and the Catholics "Romans" or "Papists." If not, they say: "We admit that you are Catholic, but so are we." But the *sensus communis* does not allow itself though all this to be misled one iota. Ask the first non-Catholic child where the

Catholic Church is in a given place, or whether he himself is a Catholic, and, *nolens volens*, he will give witness to the truth with his answer. Unerringly, inexorably, the common judgment of the world calls the Catholic Church by her true name. That is why it cannot now or ever in the future call what is limited by space and time—Arianism, Lutheranism, Anglicanism, and so on—universal, general, Catholic.

With these further references, the full weight of the statement of the great Bishop of Hippo that has already been cited cannot be escaped. And St. Augustine expressed the same thought in another place as well:

> We must be in communion with that Church which is Catholic and which will be called Catholic not only by all of her children, but also by all of her enemies. For even heretics and schismatics, despite themselves, when they are speaking not among themselves but with outsiders, do not call the Catholic Church anything other than the Catholic Church. Neither would they be understood should they not call her by the name which the whole world uses as well. (*De Vera Rel.*, c. VII)

After this, do I have to show you in all particulars that the Church that calls itself Catholic and is generally so called by those outside her community, really is Catholic? From the days when Christ the Lord commanded the Apostles to go out into the whole world to teach and to baptize all nations, she has obeyed this command continuously, through all times and through all lands of the known world. She has spread one and the same Gospel in the languages of all peoples. It is she who from the cradle of Christendom in Asia soon conquered Europe and North Africa for the Gospel. It is she who immediately after the discovery of the New World sent her missionaries there as well. It was her missionaries who disseminated the seed of divine Truth among innumerable barbarian tribes and fertilized the ground with streams of blood. It is they who still today make conquests for the Kingdom of Christ in all realms, in all zones, in the blazing Sahara and the icy solitudes in the upper north of British America.

Examine the map of the world and count up the lands through which the children of the one, holy Church have spread out.

*{In January, 1890, the Catholic Church numbered 8 patriarchs, 150 Church Provinces, 189 Archbishops, 748 bishops, 109 Apostolic Vicariates, 39 Apostolic Prefectures, 80 titular Archdioceses and 350 titular dioceses, with more than 220 million believers. What has to be news to you is that of the almost 112 million inhabitants of America, perhaps more than half are Catholic, and of the lesser half only a relatively very insignificant lot are Lutheran. In the United States the census of 1890 attributes to them 1,231,071 "communicants." In Central and South America they are everywhere completely unknown, and it would probably be reckoning too high if one counted 3 million Lutherans—2.7%—among the whole population of the New World}.

And then: name for me one Protestant denomination that has even only just approached such a universal spread. Name for me one that can boast of even only one single people, one sole barbarian tribe in the lands that became accessible in the period after the "Reformation" that has permanently been won for its teaching!

When Protestants point to the expansion of the Catholic Church, one often hears this reproach: The extent is not what counts; a great "heap" does not matter; the Pharisees and their minions once were the majority among the People of God, But Christ the Lord complained about them, consoled His small flock, and warned of the dangers of the wide road [to Hell]. This is very true. In Christ's time His flock was actually still small. But it was obviously not His intention that this should remain so forever. He Himself had limited His worldly work to the narrow borders of a small corner of the Earth, but before His return to the Father He had deputized His messengers to go throughout the globe, to all the peoples of the Earth, and He had prophesied clearly enough in His parable of the mustard seed, whose purpose is to grow up to be a great tree, what the success of their mission should and would be.

Apart from that, one must keep in mind that no one expected the existence of a single characteristic—hence, also, neither the existence of the characteristic of catholicity on its own— as being a sufficient mark of the Church of Christ. There are a number of them, and they all stand in the closest harmony. Consider them therefore in relationship with one another, my friend; compare the one with the others and you will recognize how one expands upon and illuminates the others. If you consider the catholicity of the Church in connection with her unity, would this not become an all the more effective mark of the Church the further that Church extended in time and space? And, vice versa, does not the mark of catholicity become still more persuasive through the fact that that miraculous unity that I described for you in one of my earlier letters reigns at all times and everywhere in this so widely extended universal Church that is called Catholic by everyone?

Now probably you also believe in a Catholic Church, but an invisible one. You might think it to be at least possible that I might agree with you regarding this. But my answer, briefly, is the following: how then should someone who is looking for the Church ever find her? *I* do not have the answer, but *you* are the one who has to give it. For it is not I but you who are the one who maintains the existence of an invisible Church. Can you give me an answer; an illuminating, convincing answer?

The answer must be this. Christ founded a Church. We are supposed to hear this Church. Everyone, including the most simple-minded of all must be able to find her. Where is this Church, this teaching Church? For she must after all also be such a Church, if we are supposed to hear her. She cannot be composed of creatures of body and soul, like you and me, like Dr. Luther and your preacher, like your Consistory and your Regional Synod, if she is invisible. Is she in the thunder of a storm, or in the rustling of the wind, or, in the final analysis, in the ghostly voices of spiritualist mediums?

The Protestant theologian R. Rothe correctly says, with respect to this embarrassing little discovery of Protestantism, "The invisible Church is a *contradictio in adjecto*" (*Anfänge der christlichen Kirche*, p. 100). It is a knife without a blade, a fig leaf that is made of empty air, but with which one tries in vain to cover his nakedness. Open your eyes with confidence and you will see and hear the true Church of Christ, the "City on a Hill" that "cannot remain hidden," just as clearly and distinctly as once those to whom these words were spoken saw and heard the Lord who spoke them on the Mount.

Your H.

~Chapter 18~
Reformed Christianity vs. Apostolic Christianity

My Dear D.,

I have highlighted three marks of the Church. I now come to the last.

The true Church, last of all, must be apostolic; not a creation of post-apostolic times, not a branch that earlier or later fell off the tree that grew from the mustard seed of Jesus Christ, but that immemorial tree itself that was planted by the hand of the Lord and cultivated by the Apostles; a flock whose shepherds in unbroken succession reach back from today to the days of the Apostles; a Church that teaches and believes the same now as she did then and never has taught and believed anything else.

But nothing is clearer than that this mark is found in the Catholic Church and in her alone. In her and in her alone has the Rite of Ordination remained at all times intact. She and she alone has lawfully derived her mission and passed it on from one to another at all times. Her teachings and hers alone have never changed. There is not one single instance in the dogmatic history of the Catholic Church in which the Church has taught something that was declared heretical by her beforehand, or in which she declared something to be heretical that she had defined beforehand as dogma.

You might object to me: we also believe that we are apostolic, if not in mission, nevertheless in teaching. So now I must ask you if the Church of Christ could ever fall into error in her teaching? If you believe in the promise of Christ, it certainly could not. For He promised to remain with His Church until the end of the world (Matthew 28:20). He sent her the Spirit of Truth who would remain with her for Eternity (John 14:16) and would teach her all Truth (John 16:13). How, then, could she ever err!

147

And now, let me ask a further question, my dear friend. Did the Church generally believe before 1517 that Christ had established seven Sacraments? Was this an error? Either this was impossible or Christ had lied, for there would then have been a time in which the Spirit of the Truth had been withdrawn from the Church. The Faith that Christ has established seven Sacraments was therefore the true Faith, the Apostolic Faith. But you do not have this belief any longer; you, therefore, are in error; and there is consequently no truth to the assertion that you are, at the very least, of the Apostolic Faith. This is not true. You are not the old, apostolic Church. You have broken with this, with the one innovation that has been noted already offering a fully sufficient proof of that fact.

But has the Church not also introduced new teachings? Have we not even experienced this in our own day with the dogma of the Infallibility of the Pope? No, my good D. For neither the Infallibility of the Pope nor any other of the Catholic dogmas that you hold to be innovations are in reality something new.

You have certainly often read the saying: "*Roma locuta est, causa finita est*" [Rome has spoken; the matter is closed]. Protestants have also often cited it since Vatican Council, not infrequently when they want to try out their mockery upon us. Do you know from whence this saying comes? It comes from St. Augustine. It has the venerable age of one and one half millennia. Therefore the decision of the Roman See inside those limitations that I indicated to you earlier has already long been held as being authoritative in the Catholic Church. And this Church has never had the teaching that the Pope was *not* infallible. It is much more the opposite teaching that already before the [First] Vatican Council was presented as the sole correct one in all of the purest textbooks.

What the Vatican Council did, therefore, was in no way to propagate an innovation, but only to offer the clear, dogmatic highlighting and definition of a truth long present in the Church. Already beforehand, always and generally, the Church held it to be certain that the pope and bishops together could not err in their final decision with regard to the Faith. But up until the Vatican Council, scholars liked to argue over the question of whether the same was valid for the decisions of the pope when acting on his own. As long as this truth applied practically and also did not appear to be threatened theoretically, the Church had no reason to define the latter position universally.

The same thing holds for the truths of the Most Holy Trinity, the Divinity of Christ, and other dogmas that also were never new in the Church but were at a given time defined by her. The Church now held that the time for a definition had come and that this was necessary. Surely the pope, given the dispersal of the bishops over all five parts of the world, could no more call the whole episcopacy to Rome at the drop of a hat; perhaps, for example, on account of a false teaching of a professor, so as to avert the danger that might be provoked by this over the course of time through the decision of a Council! On the other hand, the faithful had need of certainty in such cases, as, for example, at the time of the battle over the teaching of Hermes and Günther. Therefore it was the appropriate time for the Church solemnly to define the infallibility of her spiritual Head. He who says that the teaching of Papal Infallibility is an innovation is simply muddle-headed. He confuses the substance of the dogma itself with the act of its definition.

Among such muddled heads is that handful of separatists that erroneously calls itself the Old Catholics. They believe in the infallibility of an Ecumenical Council, but not in the infallibility of the pope, even if an Ecumenical Council decides that they are wrong, which, in practice, is what happened at the Vatican Council.

Apart from that, for those who recognize in the pope the successor of Peter, the infallibility of the pope in the sense defined by the Vatican Council goes without saying as being something obvious. It is so much a consequence of the doctrine of the Primacy that even Luther (in his work, *The Papacy Founded by the Devil*) confessed that if the pope were the Supreme Head of the Church his doctrinal decisions would have to be infallible.

The one, holy, Catholic Church is also apostolic, established by Christ on the foundations of Peter and the Apostles, always the same, a teacher for all peoples and times, incapable of deceit, the true and original Church of our fathers, of Christ and the Apostles through the unbroken line of successors of 256 popes until Leo XIII. "All of the apostolic churches—Antioch, Alexandria, Jerusalem—have perished; only Rome stands. '*Quia fide vestra annuntiatur in universo mundo* [because your faith has been spoken of in the whole world],' the Apostle to the World already said of the Romans (Romans 1:8). How miraculously these words that were written at a time when the Roman Church was still a small, inconsequential mustard seed have been fulfilled!" (Hagemann, *Die Römische Kirche*, p. 693).

Some years ago I was on a visit to my good old Uncle E. in H. I have already so often spoken to you of this doughty man to whom I owe so much that you certainly will remember him. One morning, I accompanied him on his way to his office. The path led past the Catholic cathedral, and Uncle E. thought we might well go inside so that I might at least once see the interior of this venerable thousand-year-old construction.

A rather large number of people inside knelt praying, participating in the celebration of a Low Mass. When I quietly posed a question to him in the church, my uncle rebuked me for doing so in a serious but friendly way, indicating to me that it was inappropriate and likely to disturb their prayer. Afterwards, he told me that there never failed to be prayerful people there every morning, by good and bad weather, and after a rather thoughtful pause he added that he wondered whether "these people really were so deeply steeped in their faith." There was something in the tone of his voice that indicated that what he really wanted to say was: "what might it be that drew these people to church even on a weekday; was it pure piety alone, or were there also other motives behind it?" It was possible that the dark notion of a "Roman coercion of conscience" was not far from his mind.

I remembered that episode last Christmas when I went to

Mass with my wife and children. On this feast the masses begin in Catholic churches already in the quiet of the night, if possible at midnight, and then one after another until noon. No Catholic is bound to attend one of the nocturnal services. However, our Church was already so full at the first Mass that an apple could not fall to the ground inside it. Go yourself and you will see the same thing wherever you might be. Despite the fact that the winter might be raw and stormy, the way to Church both long and blocked by snow, this will not keep a Catholic that easily from celebrating the holy night in the house of God.

I saw among the devout crowd at this last holiday as at earlier ones many weak old men next to the glowing faces of tender children; pampered ladies next to weather-beaten workers; people of all classes and every age: all united in the deepest devotion before the altar of the Most High and the Divine Child in the crib. And it was there that I thought of that episode with Uncle E. What is it that attracts all these people to church on that holy night, and all those millions throughout the entire world?

It is the same thing that once drew the shepherds in the field to Bethlehem: their firm, living, active belief in love! Just as those shepherds did not doubt a moment after the message of the angel of the great miracle of the Incarnation of God, but hurriedly rushed there to adore the newborn Redeemer, so also all these sincere Catholics. The fact that Jesus Christ is truly the Son of God, born of the Virgin Mary in the city of David, is, for them, like all the other parts of their Creed, an historical reality of incontrovertible certainty. And where such a certainty of belief lives in the hearts of men, how could it be otherwise than that it would fire hearts to deep love and to joyful exertion especially on that holy night!

It is the same faith, and nothing else, that also draws many Catholics in the entire world to their churches, like those in H., even on weekdays. These are in reality and completely the houses of God because God Himself really and completely lives in them. No command of the Church, no coercion of conscience, no other motive induces them to go there; only their firm, lively, loving faith; that sentiment with which our Schiller in *Gang nach dem Einsenhammer* has Fridolin speak and act upon: "Do not avoid the good Lord, find him on your path."

But from whence comes this certainty of belief that excludes every shadow of a doubt; a faith shared by the child and the old, the poor and the rich, the learned and the unlearned in the same manner? My dear D., it comes from the fact that this faith does not sway in the wind for the Catholic like any merely objective truth, but because it rests for him and in him on a firm, unshakeable foundation. In other words, because the principle from which his belief is formed, in contrast to the formal principle of Protestantism, is rational to the highest degree.

The Catholic believes not on the basis of his own insight, and also not on that of the dead, dumb, text of the Bible; or, much more accurately, whatever he or some preacher or some insignificant synod thinks to be found therein. Rather, he believes what God has revealed, and because God has revealed it. What God has revealed he knows through the Catholic Church that was founded by God. And it is the Word of God and the history of the Church, along with the marks that her Divine Founder imprinted unmistakably upon her, that testify to him that this Church was founded by God and is the infallible herald of His Revelation.

This, my friend, is the source of the undoubting, living faith of the Catholic. It is on this unshakeable, firm foundation that it rests. However nicely you may speak of faith in Protestantism, truly, you have no concept of the Catholic certainty of faith, and you cannot have it precisely because your Creed lacks the firm justification, indeed the keystone of this faith: namely, the one, holy, catholic and apostolic Church; she who stands before us Catholics as full of light and life as the angel of God in the holy night stood before the eyes of the shepherds of Bethlehem.

Protestantism has placed the Bible—unobserved, or rather whatever best fits its business—in the place of the Church. If, nevertheless you also, at least still with your lips, confess there to be "one holy Christian Church," someone conceives of this

Church in a certain way, someone else in another, and a third in simply no way at all. And that could not be otherwise. For if a Protestant appealing to these words really would unite together with them clearly defined concepts, then he, as a Protestant could not actually believe in them. A look at his so-called Church would belie his confession of faith.

What actually is this "Church?" "It is like an officer's corps without an army behind it, followed instead only by small groups of troops, weak and ragged, almost helpless, engaged in a great deal of often intense work and yet remaining far behind the overwhelming power of its opponent." One of its main spokesmen in its land of birth, the Court Preacher Adalbert Stöcker, characterized it this way just recently in his *Deutsche Evangelische Kirchenzeitung* (mid-December, 1894). And this weak, ragged, almost helpless rabble is supposed to be the one, holy, Church of Christ, the fundamental pillar of truth, the unmistakable herald of the divine Revelation to which all men are obliged to give hearing?! What a stupendous and stupid impertinence!

I have now, my dear D., traced out for you, in a cursory outline, the Church of Jesus Christ as she is in reality, as well as I am able, with my modest knowledge and ability, in the meager hours that my professional work has left over for me to do so. Oh, if only I could show you how I myself see her, how you would immediately be convinced of her divinity, how you would love her! And yet I myself only know her so late in the day, perhaps like a budding art student knows the highest of all masterpieces of the human hand. I still find and admire new things in her that bond me to her yet further, and learn to penetrate and better value everything in her more profoundly.

Those "ideals," my friend, that once, in our distant youth, "swelled the inebriated heart" have melted away for me, and probably also for you: they were foggy visions, fantastic will-o-the-wisps, ephemeral, deceptive. I however have found—and praise the mercy of God alone for this—the genuine, abiding ideal, the eternal source of all things true, good and beautiful, the "one pearl of great price" in the golden frame of the one, holy,

Catholic and apostolic Church that just as certainly embraces all of them for us on Earth as for the blessed in Heaven. All the other so-called ideals deceive and only leave receding behind them nothing other than melancholy and agitation in poor human hearts. Here, however, in the face of the true ideal, in the certain possession of that ideal, how filled the soul is with a joy and miraculous peace that it never imagined possible!

You may, my friend, indeed have still many questions to ask with respect to individual doctrines and institutions of this Church if you recognize Protestantism as the work of men and the Catholic Church as that of God. But as a rational man you will certainly not call this into question: if God had founded a Church, if it was His will that all men should hear this Church, if you are convinced that this Church is the Catholic Church, then there will be no more choice for you than that you must also submit to this Church and hear her.

The questions that may perhaps remain can obviously chang absolutely nothing regarding this obligation, just as little as possible difficulties and sacrifices that are linked together with the fulfillment of this duty. If the Catholic Church is the Institute for the Redemption of Christ, the teacher and custodian of the divine truths of Revelation, it goes without saying that all the institutions and doctrines of this Church are holy and divine, true and reasonable, all the same if you already recognize these doctrines and institutions as such or not. And, my friend, it is on account of this that I have lingered so long on the marks of the Church: so as to prove to you, with the help of God, that the Catholic Church is really the Church of Christ. This is the question of questions; the all-decisive question. If this is resolved, if the will of the questioner has said "yes" and "amen" to its resolution, then all of the perhaps still remaining questions do not any longer offer the least difficulty.

It has grown late as I have worked on this letter. Outside, the midnight bells are ringing in the New Year; 1895 A.D. Will this year bring to you, my friend, peace and true happiness? Will it lead you home to the mother abandoned by your and my forefathers?

Some have compared the Catholic Church to one of those elaborate windows in old cathedrals. The outsider distinguishes neither form nor color, but the insider is shown a tableau of sublime beauty that is rich in color and in form. It is the sunlight that reveals this beauty to the eye of the beholder. And so it is that light from above, the light of divine grace, must also illuminate the divine artwork of the Church in order to uncloak its sublime beauty to the beholder. The outsider may suspect it, he may from descriptions of it have a dark notion of it, yet only like the man born blind might have a notion of colors; he can only see it in its fullness after he has himself entered into the interior of its sanctuary.

And so also the best picture of the Church that the Catholic apologist can place before the eyes of the non-Catholic will often be no more than such a cathedral window as offered from the outside. What is missing to him is precisely what the picture depicts, the transcendent light of heaven, and the correct standpoint; that is only gained from the interior of the temple. In the case of favorable conditions, the apologist may awaken an inkling, an inkling that in the end indeed there may be "more behind" the picture; under favorable conditions a longing completely "to get behind it." The power of the apologist can have no further effect. What goes further lies in the hand of someone Higher. With a beam of His heavenly light, that which just now appeared to be confused and dark to the man sensing it and full of longing for it will shine forth to him in the purest harmony and most complete clarity.   Oh, that you might experience this, my dear D., this miraculous hour in which you, as once I myself, may have the blindfold of error completely fall from your eyes. And you, with wondrous delight, may find yourself once again in the interior of the sanctuary, in the face of eternal truth, insofar as this is granted to us mortals to see it.

In love and loyalty, your H.